The Money Mind

The Money Mind

Why Habits, Emotions, and Beliefs Matter More Than Income

Nico Farouq

Mindful Pages

Published in 2025

ISBN: 9789371775953 (PB)
ISBN: 9789371773805 (eBook)

Published by

Mindful Pages
Imprint of Alpha Editions LLC
312 W. 2nd St #1834
Casper, WY 82601, USA

Content

Introduction The Mind Behind the Money viii

Chapter 1 The Illusion of Rational Money 1

Chapter 2 Inherited Scripts 20

Chapter 3 The Emotional Economy 38

Chapter 4 The Culture of Consumption 55

Chapter 5 Self-Sabotage and Financial Loops 72

Chapter 6 The Hidden Logic of Saving and Spending 88

Chapter 7 The Psychology of Debt 106

Chapter 8 Money and Identity 122

Chapter 9 Rewriting the Money Mind 138

Chapter 10 Habits of Wealth Beyond Income 156

Chapter 11 A Different Kind of Rich 174

About the Author 192

Introduction
The Mind Behind the Money

Money has long been regarded as the ultimate measure of success, stability, and freedom. Yet, for all its prominence in our lives, it remains one of the most misunderstood forces shaping human behaviour. We often imagine that financial wellbeing is dictated by numbers alone: how much is earned, how carefully it is budgeted, how wisely it is invested. This perspective suggests that the key to prosperity lies in mastering the arithmetic of money. And yet, if that were true, we would not find high-income professionals struggling with credit card debt, nor would we see modest earners quietly building fortunes through quiet consistency. The paradox is everywhere, and it forces us to confront an unsettling truth: income is not destiny.

Our financial lives are not governed by calculators or spreadsheets but by hidden currents of thought, habit, and emotion. What drives one person to save compulsively while another spends recklessly has less to do with external circumstances and far more to do with internal scripts—those invisible stories we inherit from childhood, absorb from culture, and reinforce through our own choices. These scripts whisper to us in subtle, persistent ways: *Money is scarce, you must hoard it. Money is abundant, spend freely before it disappears. Money proves your worth, so show the world what you have.* They are rarely spoken aloud, yet they shape every transaction, every decision, and every dream we attach to money.

This book begins with the conviction that the real determinant of financial outcomes is not the size of one's paycheque, but the architecture of one's mind. Habits, emotions, and beliefs form the blueprint of our "money mind"—the largely unconscious framework that dictates how we engage with wealth, debt, saving, and spending. When this framework is distorted, no amount of income can guarantee security. When it is understood and reshaped, even modest means can yield freedom and abundance.

Why Rethinking Money Matters Now

The cultural conversation around money often oscillates between technical instruction and motivational slogans. On one end, financial advice is reduced to interest rates, retirement accounts, and investment vehicles, as if success were merely a matter of choosing the right spreadsheet formula. On the other, we hear simplistic affirmations urging us to "think rich" or "manifest abundance," as though mindset alone could erase structural realities. What is often missing is a nuanced recognition of how the psychological and emotional dimensions of money operate alongside external circumstances to produce outcomes.

Consider the recent global shifts: rising living costs, widening inequality, and a culture of instant consumption fuelled by technology. More people than ever are financially literate—they know how to calculate compound interest, they can recite the tenets of budgeting, and they are aware of the dangers of credit card debt. Yet literacy does not translate to behaviour. The gulf between knowing and doing has never been wider. We live in a society where many earn well but still feel perpetually insecure, where social media fuels constant comparison, and where the symbols of wealth often become more important than its substance. Against this backdrop, understanding the *mind behind the money* is not simply useful; it is essential.

The Unseen Patterns

Every reader brings to this subject a unique history. Some grew up in households where money was a source of constant anxiety, every purchase weighed against fear of scarcity. Others grew up in abundance but found that excess created its own distortions—entitlement, avoidance, or reckless indulgence. Still others experienced silence around money: it was never discussed, as though it were a taboo topic. Each of these backgrounds plants seeds that grow into lifelong financial patterns.

The economist may speak of rational actors and efficient markets, but daily human behaviour consistently proves otherwise. We make decisions driven by shame, by pride, by the need to belong, by the fear of missing out. We overspend to soothe stress, or underspend because security feels perpetually threatened. We avoid looking at bills because shame looms larger than numbers. These patterns do not yield to logic alone; they require recognition, compassion, and deliberate re-scripting.

A Different Lens on Wealth

To understand money properly, we must first redefine what we mean by wealth. If wealth is merely accumulation, then the highest earners should always be the most secure and content. But countless examples disprove this assumption. A schoolteacher who lives modestly may retire with ample savings, while a surgeon with a seven-figure income may find themselves trapped in a cycle of debt and overcommitment. The difference is not professional status or numerical earnings, but mindset: how each individual interprets, values, and directs the flow of money.

Wealth, as argued in these pages, is better understood as sufficiency plus choice—the capacity to live in alignment with one's values, to weather uncertainty without collapse, and to see money as a tool rather than a tyrant. Achieving this form of wealth does not begin with external strategies but with internal clarity.

The Questions This Book Confronts

At its core, this work addresses questions that every individual, regardless of income level, must eventually face:

Why do intelligent, well-educated people make financial decisions that undermine their long-term wellbeing?

Why does more income often fail to eliminate stress or insecurity?

Why do we repeat destructive financial patterns, even when we recognise them?

And most importantly, how can we break free from the hidden scripts that keep us trapped?

Each chapter that follows illuminates a different dimension of the money mind. We will examine the illusion of rationality, exploring why intelligence does not guarantee wise financial behaviour. We will trace the inherited scripts of childhood and uncover how parental silence, fear, or indulgence leaves lasting imprints. We will delve into the emotional economy, showing how spending and saving often serve as proxies for identity, validation, or comfort. We will confront the cultural machine of consumption, with its relentless demands for display and comparison. And we will explore how patterns of self-sabotage and debt form loops that eventually solidify into identities.

But this is not simply a diagnostic exercise. Beyond understanding lies transformation. Later chapters will show how awareness, mindfulness, and new habits can rewrite destructive patterns, creating a healthier relationship with money. By redefining reward, reframing debt, and designing better defaults, readers can begin to cultivate financial lives that reflect not fear or compulsion, but autonomy and meaning.

Why This Approach Is Different

You may have read books promising budgeting techniques, investment hacks, or step-by-step strategies to financial independence. These tools have their place, but they address only the surface. They are like prescribing a new diet without understanding why a person overeats, or recommending exercise routines without examining why someone avoids movement in the first place. Without addressing the underlying beliefs and emotional triggers, external tactics remain fragile.

This book takes a different stance. It does not ignore numbers, but it insists that numbers are only the visible tip of a much deeper iceberg. Beneath every financial decision lies an invisible equation of fear, desire, memory, and belief. Until that equation is acknowledged and rebalanced, no income level will suffice.

The Urgency of Change

The stakes of ignoring the money mind are profound. Financial stress remains one of the leading causes of anxiety, marital conflict, and even physical illness. It dictates where people live, what opportunities they can pursue, and how much freedom they feel over their lives. Yet financial stress does not discriminate by income bracket; it is as common among the affluent as it is among the struggling. The urgency is not merely economic but existential: how we relate to money profoundly shapes the quality of our lives.

There is also a generational dimension. Our scripts do not end with us; they are transmitted, often unconsciously, to children and communities. A household marked by secrecy around money can raise another generation equally paralysed by avoidance. A culture obsessed with display can normalise debt as a badge of belonging. To rewrite one's money mind is therefore not only a personal act of liberation but also a legacy, altering the financial culture passed forward.

Entering the Work

This introduction is not a preamble to a quick fix. It is an invitation to look with honesty and courage at the forces that govern our financial lives. Some of these forces are comforting; others may be uncomfortable to confront. But in bringing them into awareness, we create the possibility of choice. For it is only when we see the invisible scripts that we can begin to rewrite them.

The chapters that follow are organised to guide you from recognition to reconstruction. We begin by dismantling myths—the illusion that intelligence guarantees wise choices, or that income alone dictates destiny. We then move to the roots, exploring childhood scripts and emotional triggers. From there, we widen the lens to include cultural forces, cycles of self-sabotage, and the hidden logic of saving and debt. Finally, we turn towards possibility: how to cultivate habits of wealth beyond income, redefine success, and leave a legacy of healthier financial culture.

This is the map, but the journey is yours. As you read, you may recognise fragments of your own story: the stress of bills, the thrill of a purchase, the quiet shame of avoidance, the pride of saving, the confusion of contradiction. Allow these recognitions not to condemn but to illuminate. They are evidence that you are not alone, that these patterns are widely shared, and that they can be changed.

A Promise to the Reader

If you engage with the ideas here openly, you will not merely gain insights into why you spend, save, or sabotage. You will acquire a new lens through which to interpret your financial life—one that restores agency, clarity, and possibility. You will come to see money not as an external master but as an internal mirror, reflecting the habits, emotions, and beliefs you hold. And you will learn how to reshape that reflection into one that aligns with your values and aspirations.

This is the promise of *The Money Mind*: not a manual of tactics, but a guide to transformation. It does not tell you what to think, but how to see. It equips you not just to manage money, but to understand it as a living dialogue between numbers and narrative, between external circumstance and inner meaning.

You stand at the threshold of a different kind of financial literacy—one that measures wealth not merely in pounds or possessions, but in peace, autonomy, and purpose. Let us begin.

Chapter 1
The Illusion of Rational Money

We like to imagine ourselves as rational beings, carefully weighing options, calculating trade-offs, and making decisions that maximise our wellbeing. Money, in particular, seems to invite the fantasy of rationality. The image of the economically rational actor—deliberate, logical, always acting in self-interest—has dominated both classical economics and popular discourse for decades. Yet when we examine how people actually live with money, a very different picture emerges. Intelligence, education, and even financial literacy often fail to shield people from missteps. Highly accomplished professionals find themselves living from paycheque to paycheque, despite incomes that would appear to guarantee security. Meanwhile, individuals of modest means manage to achieve long-term stability and freedom. The dissonance between what we assume about rational decision-making and what actually occurs in real financial lives is striking. This chapter examines that gap, and it begins with an uncomfortable but necessary truth: when it comes to money, human beings are far less rational than they like to believe.

One of the most perplexing realities of modern financial life is that *smart people make "dumb" choices.* A surgeon with years of education and a six-figure salary may struggle under the weight of credit card debt, unable to resist the temptation of luxury goods, expensive holidays, or lifestyle inflation that rises in lockstep with income. At the same time, a primary school teacher, earning a fraction of that income, may retire decades later with a paid-off home, a well-padded pension, and the serenity of financial independence. The surgeon knew, in principle, the mathematics of debt and interest. The teacher may never have opened a finance textbook. Yet the outcomes are reversed. The explanation is not a matter of intellect but of behaviour—of how biases, emotions, and hidden beliefs shape what we do with the resources in our hands. Cognitive science tells us that human decision-making is less a clean equation than a collision between reason and impulse. Behavioural economics has catalogued dozens of biases that tilt us away from rationality: present bias, which leads us to overvalue immediate rewards and undervalue future benefits; loss aversion, which makes the pain of loss loom larger than the pleasure of gain; confirmation bias, which encourages us to seek information that supports what we already want to believe. These forces do not spare the highly intelligent. In fact, intelligence sometimes makes them more adept at rationalising poor decisions. A doctor might justify overspending by reminding themselves of the stress of their profession; a lawyer might convince themselves that luxury is a rightful reward for hard work. The mental gymnastics are subtle but powerful.

This is why financial literacy programmes, while valuable, often fail to produce lasting change. Knowledge of compound interest does not prevent someone from taking on crippling debt if the emotional pull of immediate gratification feels overwhelming. Understanding the mathematics of saving does not automatically make saving a consistent practice if one's habits are shaped by childhood scarcity or the need for social validation. To assume that knowledge alone can transform financial behaviour is to misread the human condition.

This brings us to the cultural myth that income determines destiny. Across societies, there is a widespread assumption that more money naturally leads to more stability, more happiness, and less stress. Advertisements, financial media, and even casual conversation perpetuate the belief that "if only I earned a little more, things would finally feel secure." And yet evidence persistently contradicts this assumption. Studies of subjective wellbeing consistently show that beyond a certain threshold—sufficient to meet basic needs and provide moderate comfort—additional income yields diminishing returns on happiness. People earning vastly different salaries often report similar levels of financial anxiety. A family earning £40,000 may worry about paying the mortgage, while a family earning £200,000 may lie awake at night calculating the cost of private schooling, second homes, and maintaining appearances among affluent peers. The stress is not erased by the extra zeros; it is merely reframed. In fact, higher incomes often intensify pressure, as expectations expand and lifestyles adjust. What once felt like abundance quickly becomes normal, and soon even that feels insufficient.

The myth of income as destiny is particularly damaging because it distracts people from addressing the true drivers of financial wellbeing. If the problem is assumed to be insufficient income, the solution always seems to be to earn more—work longer hours, chase promotions, launch side ventures. Yet without addressing the underlying behaviours and beliefs, higher income simply magnifies existing problems. Debt grows in proportion to earnings, savings remain elusive, and stress persists. The problem is not how much comes in, but what the mind does with it.

Here lies the real hidden variable: the "money mind." Every individual carries a set of habits, emotions, and beliefs that operate beneath conscious awareness, shaping their relationship with money. This hidden force influences whether they save or spend, whether they view money as a source of safety or as a symbol of status, whether they approach it with curiosity or with fear. It is not the size of one's salary that dictates outcomes, but the architecture of this money mind. Left unexamined, it quietly directs decisions that lead to cycles of insecurity or stability, debt or freedom. The challenge—and the opportunity—is that the money mind is not fixed. It can be recognised, interrogated, and reshaped.

The contrast between outcomes is starkly illustrated by countless real-world examples. Consider again the schoolteacher and the surgeon. The teacher may have internalised early on the value of living within one's means, setting aside a portion of each paycheque, and avoiding unnecessary debt. These behaviours, compounded over decades, yield substantial wealth. The surgeon, by contrast, may have grown up with an unspoken script equating money with status and consumption, fuelling a compulsion to display success through material symbols. Despite a far higher income, the surgeon's financial reality may be precarious, perpetually dependent on the next paycheque. The contradiction is not unusual. Across industries and professions, there are modest earners who thrive and affluent earners who flounder. The difference is rarely explained by external variables alone.

The illusion of rational money is precisely that—an illusion. To believe that intelligence ensures financial wisdom, or that income guarantees stability, is to ignore the complexity of human psychology. What this chapter offers is not a dismissal of rationality altogether but a call to expand our understanding. Rationality matters, but it is only part of the equation. Unless we recognise the biases, scripts, and emotions that shape our behaviour, rationality remains an aspiration rather than a practice. By dismantling the myth of income as destiny and exposing the hidden role of the money mind, we open the way for a more accurate, compassionate, and transformative approach to financial wellbeing.

The pages ahead will explore this illusion in depth. We will look at why intelligence and education fail to protect against poor financial decisions, and why emotions often override logic. We will examine how the cultural fixation on income obscures the deeper truths of financial security. We will introduce the framework of the money mind, showing how it explains contradictions that defy conventional wisdom. And we will ground these ideas in concrete examples, highlighting the paradoxes that surround us every day: the teacher who retires wealthy, the surgeon who drowns in debt, the entrepreneur who squanders a windfall, the shop assistant who builds a quiet fortune. Each case points to the same conclusion: money outcomes are not the product of income alone, but of the mind that governs it.

To engage with this chapter is to confront assumptions many of us have long held unquestioned. It is to recognise that our financial struggles or successes are not reflections of intelligence, morality, or fate, but of patterns that can be seen and changed. The illusion of rational money is a powerful one, but it is also liberating once exposed. For when we see that our financial future does not hinge solely on what we earn, but on how we think, feel, and act with money, we discover the possibility of control that is both more profound and more achievable than any spreadsheet could offer.

Why Smart People Make "Dumb" Choices

It is one of the most disconcerting paradoxes of modern financial life: the very people we expect to be immune to poor money decisions—those with advanced education, professional success, or enviable salaries—are often the same individuals who find themselves trapped in cycles of debt, anxiety, and fragile financial foundations. Bankers earning six-figure bonuses live month to month, consultants with postgraduate degrees juggle multiple credit cards, and doctors nearing retirement suddenly confront the reality that decades of high income have not translated into long-term security. Intelligence and financial literacy, it turns out, do not guarantee financial health. The dissonance between what people know and what they do with money reveals something profound about human behaviour: knowledge may inform, but it is emotion and bias that often decide.

The financial lives of high earners provide some of the clearest demonstrations of this truth. Consider the professional couple with household earnings exceeding £200,000 annually, yet both privately admitting they feel constantly stretched, perpetually behind, and anxious about the future. Their outgoings rise in lockstep with income: private schooling, a larger home, holidays abroad, and subtle lifestyle enhancements that quickly become non-negotiable. Despite appearances of affluence, they are as vulnerable to financial shocks as families on far lower incomes. Their predicament is not born of ignorance—they understand interest rates, pension contributions, and mortgage terms—but of psychology. Each financial choice is influenced by hidden drivers: the desire to keep pace with peers, the emotional relief of retail therapy after stressful workdays, the unconscious assumption that tomorrow's income will always be greater than today's.

This disjunction between knowledge and behaviour has been carefully studied by behavioural economists and psychologists alike. Traditional economics assumes that human beings are rational actors who weigh costs and benefits to maximise utility. Reality, however, consistently contradicts this model. Instead of rationality, we see patterns of cognitive bias, short-termism, and emotional distortion. *Present bias* leads people to prioritise immediate gratification over distant benefits, even when they intellectually recognise the long-term cost. This is why a professional who understands compound interest may still raid their retirement savings for a holiday or a new car. *Loss aversion* means that the fear of losing money is psychologically more powerful than the prospect of equivalent gains, leading people to hold on to poor investments longer than logic dictates, or to resist necessary adjustments because admitting loss feels unbearable. Intelligence does not eliminate these biases; it often amplifies them, as smart individuals construct elaborate rationalisations to defend irrational behaviour.

Another significant factor is the emotional context in which money decisions are made. Financial stress, even among high earners, narrows decision-making bandwidth. When anxiety is heightened, the brain shifts into short-term survival mode, prioritising immediate relief over longer-term strategy. A lawyer facing punishing hours and overwhelming pressure may convince themselves that expensive conveniences—a costly car service, frequent dining out, designer clothes—are justified rewards for enduring stress. These choices, while temporarily soothing, compound financial strain. Similarly, individuals in high-status professions often experience identity pressures: spending is not simply about utility but about signalling competence, success, and belonging within their professional or social circle. The irony is stark: those who can afford more are often trapped by the compulsion to prove they belong among those who can afford most.

Historical and contemporary examples illustrate the point vividly. Professional athletes, who earn in a few years what many people would not see in a lifetime, are notorious for experiencing financial collapse within a decade of retirement. Despite access to advisors and the intellectual capacity to grasp the numbers, many succumb to spending habits, entourages, or risky investments that devour fortunes. At the other end of the spectrum, teachers, nurses, or civil servants with comparatively modest wages frequently retire with solid financial stability. The difference lies less in what they knew about finance than in how consistently they acted upon modest but steady principles—living within their means, saving regularly, and resisting the pull of status-driven consumption.

To label these disparities as mere discipline or recklessness is to oversimplify. What drives them is the invisible architecture of belief and emotion—the "money mind" that shapes behaviour before reason can intervene. For the high earner conditioned to equate money with self-worth, restraint feels like deprivation. For the modest earner who associates security with prudence, saving is not a burden but a reassurance. These contrasting orientations are not functions of IQ or education; they are scripts internalised through family culture, personal experience, and societal expectation. Once embedded, they exert more power over financial outcomes than any abstract knowledge of economics.

One particularly revealing phenomenon is lifestyle inflation. As income grows, so too do expectations. The promotion that doubles a salary is rarely followed by doubling of savings; instead, expenditures expand to match the new normal. A larger home seems necessary, holidays become more extravagant, and consumer goods are upgraded as though they were entitlements rather than luxuries. The psychological mechanism at play is *hedonic adaptation*—the tendency to quickly adjust to new circumstances so that what once felt extraordinary becomes ordinary. Intelligence offers no shield from this process. In fact, those with higher incomes are often more exposed to it, because opportunities for consumption multiply with each pay rise, while the discipline to hold spending steady requires conscious resistance against the pull of habit and social comparison.

The most unsettling insight is that financial self-sabotage often masquerades as rationality. A professional might insist that their spending is justified because they "work hard" or because "life is short." Another might argue that investing in status goods is strategic networking, a way of projecting success to attract clients or opportunities. These rationalisations blur the line between legitimate reasoning and emotional appeasement. They are persuasive precisely because they contain fragments of truth, yet they ultimately distort long-term wellbeing. What looks like a rational decision from the inside often appears irrational when viewed through the lens of outcomes.

Yet the paradox of smart people making "dumb" financial choices should not be read as a moral failing. It is, in fact, a profoundly human phenomenon. The very qualities that enable intelligence—creativity, imagination, the ability to justify and interpret—also enable the construction of compelling narratives that defend poor behaviour. It is not stupidity but misapplied intelligence that often leads to fragility. Recognising this shifts the frame: the challenge is not simply to become smarter, but to become more aware of the biases and emotions that accompany intelligence.

The practical implications are significant. For high earners, acknowledging the limits of rationality is the first step towards financial health. It means recognising that knowledge of compound interest will not, on its own, prevent overspending; that awareness of debt dynamics does not erase the allure of indulgence; and that income alone does not guarantee security. It requires cultivating habits and systems that counteract bias rather than relying on willpower. Automatic savings, spending friction, and accountability mechanisms are not crutches for the ignorant; they are safeguards for the intelligent, designed to prevent the rational mind from being overwhelmed by emotional impulse.

At the heart of this paradox lies a deeper philosophical truth: money decisions are never purely economic. They are expressions of identity, emotion, and belief, enacted through numbers but rooted in psychology. To understand why smart people make "dumb" financial choices is to acknowledge that intelligence without self-awareness is insufficient. Financial health is less a test of intellect than of alignment—between knowledge and action, values and behaviour, intention and habit. Until that alignment is achieved, even the brightest minds will remain vulnerable to choices that undermine their long-term wellbeing.

The lesson is humbling, but also liberating. If poor financial outcomes are not solely the product of ignorance, then they are not inevitable. They reflect patterns that can be recognised, interrogated, and reshaped. The surgeon in debt and the teacher in surplus are not anomalies but illustrations of a broader truth: what determines financial health is not what we know, but how we live what we know. Intelligence sets the stage, but the performance is directed by bias, emotion, and the scripts of the money mind. To see this clearly is the beginning of genuine financial wisdom.

The Myth of Income as Destiny

Few ideas are as deeply embedded in modern culture as the conviction that more money inevitably leads to more security, more freedom, and greater happiness. The notion that income alone dictates destiny is so pervasive that it underpins not only personal aspirations but also public policy, advertising, and collective measures of success. Parents urge children towards high-paying careers on the assumption that financial stability will follow; governments equate rising average incomes with progress; individuals chase salary increases as the primary marker of achievement. Yet when we scrutinise lived experience, the myth quickly begins to unravel. A growing body of research reveals that people earning vastly different amounts often report strikingly similar levels of stress, insecurity, and dissatisfaction. The assumption that a higher paycheque automatically insulates against financial worry is less a truth than a cultural illusion.

The most compelling evidence against the income-destiny equation is found in the phenomenon of lifestyle inflation. As people earn more, their expenses expand to match or exceed the new income. The raise that promised relief from financial pressure often evaporates into upgraded homes, cars, holidays, and habits. What once felt like luxury swiftly becomes baseline. This process—known as *hedonic adaptation*—ensures that even as income rises, the subjective sense of sufficiency does not. A family that moves from a modest home into a larger one may briefly experience delight, but soon the larger mortgage, increased upkeep, and social comparisons within a wealthier neighbourhood generate new anxieties. The same cycle repeats at higher levels of income, creating a treadmill effect in which the horizon of "enough" constantly recedes.

Studies from behavioural economics reinforce this observation. Research by Daniel Kahneman and Angus Deaton, widely cited for its examination of income and wellbeing, demonstrated that beyond a certain threshold—roughly $75,000 in the United States at the time of their study—additional income had little effect on day-to-day emotional wellbeing. Higher earnings did improve life evaluations when people looked at their circumstances abstractly, but the quality of everyday mood, stress levels, and emotional stability plateaued. This finding has been echoed in multiple contexts: once basic needs and modest comforts are covered, the psychological benefits of additional income diminish sharply. Yet despite this evidence, cultural narratives continue to frame income as the decisive variable separating financial suffering from security.

The persistence of the myth is partly explained by the social function of money. In many professional and social environments, income operates less as a tool for meeting needs and more as a proxy for status. A lawyer earning £150,000 may feel insecure when surrounded by colleagues on £250,000, even though they enjoy a lifestyle far beyond subsistence. The stress is not derived from absolute scarcity but from *relative standing*. Social comparison theory, first articulated by Leon Festinger, helps explain this: people assess their own situation not in isolation but by measuring themselves against those around them. This comparison often leads to dissatisfaction, regardless of objective wealth. Thus, a professional at the upper end of the national income scale may feel poorer than they are because they measure themselves against an even higher-income reference group.

Real-world examples highlight the contradictions vividly. Financial advisers often observe surgeons or senior executives with incomes well into six figures struggling under significant debt burdens, while schoolteachers or librarians with comparatively modest salaries retire comfortably. The difference lies not in opportunity but in orientation. The high-income individual may see their salary as a mandate to spend, aligning their lifestyle with cultural expectations of success. The modest earner may adopt habits of restraint and long-term planning, focusing on security rather than display. These contrasting behaviours expose the fragility of assuming that earnings guarantee financial stability. Income provides potential, but the translation of potential into outcomes is mediated by habits, emotions, and beliefs.

Cultural narratives further entrench the myth by equating material accumulation with fulfilment. Advertising industries thrive on the promise that the next purchase, enabled by the next raise, will deliver satisfaction. This conditioning begins early and rarely faces direct challenge. As a result, many individuals come to believe that income growth is the only path to security or self-worth. Yet when expectations and consumption rise in tandem, the very act of earning more can deepen stress rather than relieve it. Research on consumer debt consistently shows that debt levels increase across income brackets; higher earners are not exempt. Indeed, credit access often expands with income, making it easier to borrow larger sums. What should provide safety instead becomes another source of vulnerability.

Another reason the income myth endures is that it contains a kernel of truth. Income does matter, especially at lower levels where financial scarcity imposes constant stress. The difference between subsistence and stability is stark, and additional income in these ranges can significantly improve wellbeing. What the myth gets wrong is extrapolating this principle indefinitely, assuming that if some income helps, more must always help more. The nuance is critical: while income provides diminishing returns after basic needs are met, cultural discourse rarely acknowledges the plateau. People are left believing that security remains just one promotion away, even if evidence shows that the promised relief rarely arrives.

Philosophically, the belief in income as destiny reflects a broader modern faith in quantifiable metrics. In a culture obsessed with measurement—test scores, productivity targets, GDP—income offers a clean number to signal worth. It is easier to tally than emotional wellbeing, relational health, or alignment with values. The danger lies in mistaking the measurable for the meaningful. Financial outcomes are complex, shaped not only by earnings but by spending patterns, saving habits, emotional resilience, and the stories people tell themselves about money. By focusing narrowly on income, we neglect the subtler but more decisive factors that determine whether financial lives feel stable or fragile.

Consider also the intergenerational implications. Many families push children towards lucrative fields on the assumption that high earnings guarantee a good life. Yet the reality is that careers demanding high incomes often bring higher stress, longer hours, and narrower margins for error. A high earner saddled with debt and anxiety may envy the relative serenity of a modest earner who lives with greater intentionality. The myth of income as destiny not only distorts individual expectations but also shapes generational pathways, perpetuating the belief that financial wellbeing can be secured by chasing the largest paycheque available.

The contemporary economic environment magnifies these tensions. Rising costs of housing, healthcare, and education mean that even high incomes do not stretch as far as they once did. Professionals in urban centres may earn salaries that appear extravagant by national standards yet still feel perpetually squeezed. The mismatch between earnings and outgoings highlights a deeper truth: financial stress is not eradicated by crossing a specific income threshold. It persists because it is driven by more than numbers—it is shaped by perceptions of adequacy, cultural pressures, and psychological habits.

Challenging the myth of income as destiny requires not dismissing the value of earnings but reframing their role. Income is a resource, not a guarantee. It provides the opportunity for stability, but whether that opportunity is realised depends on choices, behaviours, and beliefs. Understanding this distinction is liberating, because it shifts focus from chasing higher income as the sole path to security towards cultivating healthier money minds. Recognising that more is not always better allows individuals to reclaim agency, redirecting attention from endless accumulation to deliberate alignment of money with values and goals.

Ultimately, the myth of income as destiny endures because it simplifies a complex truth. It offers a reassuringly linear equation—more income equals more security—that spares us from confronting the uncomfortable reality that money alone cannot resolve deeper anxieties. Yet liberation begins with clarity. By disentangling income from destiny, by recognising the limits of what higher pay can deliver, individuals and societies alike can reorient towards more sustainable and authentic measures of financial health. Income may shape the possibilities available, but it is the mind that determines whether those possibilities translate into freedom or fragility.

The Real Hidden Variable

At first glance, money seems to be about numbers. Income, expenses, assets, liabilities—the balance sheet appears neutral, objective, free of ambiguity. Yet beneath the arithmetic lies something far more consequential: the patterns of thought and emotion that shape how those numbers are lived out. Two people may earn the same salary and inhabit radically different financial realities. One steadily builds security, the other drifts from crisis to crisis. The divergence is not explained by figures but by psychology. What determines the outcome is not income itself, but the *money mind*—the hidden constellation of habits, beliefs, and emotions that unconsciously govern financial behaviour.

This concept reframes the way we think about financial wellbeing. Instead of assuming that success is dictated by external resources alone, it directs attention inward to the scripts and associations that quietly steer decisions. For some, money is bound up with safety, leading to compulsive saving even when circumstances allow for greater freedom. For others, money represents self-worth, fuelling spending as a way of broadcasting success. These orientations are rarely examined consciously, yet they influence choices more reliably than rational calculation. To grasp the significance of the money mind is to see that financial life is less about what we know and more about what we *carry within us*.

Consider how early experiences imprint themselves. A child who repeatedly hears "we can't afford that" may internalise scarcity so deeply that, even as an adult with a secure income, they feel anxious parting with money. They may hoard savings, delay necessary spending, or forgo opportunities because the fear of running out looms larger than reality. Another child, raised in a household where money flowed freely without visible effort, might internalise the opposite script—that resources are inexhaustible and should be enjoyed without restraint. As an adult, they may struggle with debt, convinced that tomorrow's income will always cover today's indulgence. These early lessons are rarely articulated; they are absorbed silently through observation, tone, and atmosphere. Yet they calcify into habits that persist long after the original context has vanished.

The influence of money mind extends beyond childhood conditioning. Cultural expectations also shape it in profound ways. In consumer-driven societies, the association between wealth and identity is constantly reinforced: possessions are presented as proof of belonging, status, or personal worth. Even those who intellectually reject these narratives often find themselves subtly influenced, compelled to keep pace with peers or to project success through visible consumption. Here the money mind is not merely personal but social, a product of cultural conditioning that is absorbed as naturally as language. To navigate money without recognising these forces is to risk being directed by them unconsciously.

Psychological research provides ample evidence that unconscious drivers consistently override rationality. Studies of financial behaviour show that knowledge of budgeting or investing does not reliably translate into action. A person may understand perfectly well the importance of emergency savings, yet find themselves repeatedly draining the account for discretionary spending. The obstacle is not ignorance but the emotional weight attached to money. Spending may relieve stress, express love, or signal competence. Saving may evoke pride but also anxiety, especially if money is unconsciously linked to vulnerability or fear. These emotional associations are the hidden levers of behaviour. Unless they are surfaced, logic alone will not suffice.

The money mind explains contradictions that otherwise appear baffling. Why do high earners frequently struggle with financial insecurity while modest earners thrive? Why do intelligent people make choices they know are self-defeating? Why does more income so often fail to bring more peace? The answer lies in the scripts at work. A surgeon with a seven-figure income may feel compelled to live in a neighbourhood that reflects their professional standing, to drive a car that signals success, to send children to private schools because that is what peers do. Each decision may appear rational in isolation but, taken together, leaves them financially strained. A teacher with far lower income may quietly build wealth by internalising different scripts: that security is preferable to status, that living below one's means is a source of freedom, that contentment is not measured by comparison. The disparity in outcome arises not from income but from the architecture of the money mind.

Understanding this hidden variable is not only an act of analysis but of liberation. Once we recognise that financial behaviour is shaped by unconscious scripts, we open the possibility of rewriting them. Awareness becomes the first tool: noticing patterns, identifying triggers, and asking whether the beliefs that guide us still serve us. For many, this is a radical shift. It means confronting uncomfortable truths—acknowledging that fear, shame, or pride have played larger roles in money decisions than logic. But it also means reclaiming agency. A belief inherited from childhood need not define adulthood. A cultural script absorbed uncritically can be questioned and discarded.

The money mind also offers a more compassionate lens for understanding financial struggles. Too often, poor financial outcomes are attributed to laziness, ignorance, or lack of discipline. These judgments ignore the psychological realities at play. Recognising the role of the money mind reframes the issue: people are not failing because they lack knowledge, but because they are driven by forces they have not yet identified. This perspective encourages empathy rather than blame, while still demanding accountability. It acknowledges that change is possible but requires confronting deeper layers of self-understanding.

Framing the rest of the book around the money mind is not an abstraction; it is a way of unifying diverse financial phenomena under a single explanatory principle. Debt, overspending, compulsive saving, shame, secrecy, lifestyle inflation—these are not isolated problems but expressions of the same underlying dynamics. By examining the habits, emotions, and beliefs that constitute the money mind, we create a framework broad enough to encompass varied experiences yet specific enough to guide transformation. It is the hidden variable that explains why strategies succeed for some and fail for others, why the same advice produces liberation in one person and frustration in another.

What makes the money mind so powerful is that it operates invisibly. People rarely pause to interrogate the beliefs driving their behaviour. They may be aware of their debt but not of the fear of inadequacy fuelling it. They may notice their compulsive saving but not the childhood anxiety that makes spending feel unsafe. Bringing these dynamics into view is the essential first step. Only when they are named can they be re-scripted. The remainder of this book is built on this insight: to change our financial lives, we must first understand the money mind.

The hidden variable does not determine destiny in the deterministic sense. It shapes tendencies, inclinations, and defaults. But defaults can be redesigned. The awareness that financial behaviour is not fixed, but malleable, is itself transformative. It replaces fatalism with possibility. If the problem is not ignorance but unconscious belief, then education must be paired with introspection; if the challenge is not lack of income but misaligned scripts, then the task is to rewrite those scripts with intention. The money mind is both the obstacle and the opportunity.

To see money clearly, we must look beyond the numbers to the narratives beneath them. It is there, in the hidden scripts of the money mind, that the real story unfolds. Understanding this hidden variable changes everything: it reframes financial success, explains apparent contradictions, and points towards the path of lasting change. The journey forward is not about chasing higher income or more knowledge alone. It is about transforming the internal architecture that governs what we do with what we already have.

Case Studies of Contradiction

The assumption that higher income guarantees better financial outcomes collapses quickly when we examine the lived realities of people across professions. Some of the most striking lessons come not from abstract theory but from the stark contrasts between individuals whose financial lives defy cultural expectations. These contradictions highlight the central argument of this book: money outcomes are not determined by how much flows in, but by the patterns of belief and behaviour that govern what is done with it.

Consider the case of a primary school teacher who retires comfortably at sixty-five. Over a career spanning four decades, their salary never approached six figures. They worked within the public sector, facing modest pay rises and limited opportunities for sudden windfalls. Yet they leave their career with a paid-off home, a healthy pension, and savings sufficient to support travel, hobbies, and family generosity. Their security is not the product of extraordinary luck but of consistent habits: living below their means, contributing steadily to pension funds, and resisting the cultural script that equates success with visible consumption. Importantly, their relationship with money was guided by an internalised belief in prudence and sufficiency. For them, wealth meant stability and freedom rather than endless display.

Contrast this with the life of a surgeon earning several times the teacher's salary. From early in their career, the income appears transformative: student loans are swiftly repaid, luxury is within reach, and social recognition accompanies professional status. Yet by mid-life, the surgeon feels financially cornered. A sprawling house carries a heavy mortgage, private school fees consume much of their monthly income, and multiple vehicles and holidays abroad add to the financial outflow. Despite a household income that dwarfs the national average, they live month to month, anxious about retirement and resentful of the constant need to maintain appearances. The issue is not ignorance; this individual understands basic financial principles. Rather, their habits and beliefs—equating income with entitlement, consumption with success, and status with security—have driven them into fragility. The same income that could have secured lasting freedom has instead financed perpetual insecurity.

These examples are not outliers but patterns repeated across countless professions. Teachers, librarians, and civil servants often emerge as financially stable despite modest wages, while doctors, executives, and lawyers find themselves burdened by debt and stress. The contradiction becomes even sharper when viewed through empirical research. Surveys consistently show that financial stress is not confined to low-income groups. Families earning well above median incomes frequently report living "paycheque to paycheque." Credit data confirms this: higher income households often carry larger absolute debt burdens, making them acutely vulnerable to economic shocks. Wealth is not created by earning potential alone but by how income is translated—or squandered—through behaviour.

One revealing example comes from studies of lottery winners. A sudden windfall offers the clearest possible test of the income-as-destiny assumption. Yet longitudinal research demonstrates that many lottery winners find themselves in financial distress within a few years of their prize. Their spending escalates, new social pressures emerge, and poor financial habits are amplified rather than erased. In contrast, modest earners who never experience a windfall but cultivate disciplined behaviours frequently achieve greater long-term security. The contrast underscores the same principle: *the money mind, not the money itself, dictates outcomes.*

Another instructive case can be found in entrepreneurial circles. Entrepreneurs who achieve rapid financial success often discover that their internal money scripts determine whether they retain or lose their gains. Some approach newfound wealth with caution, using it to consolidate stability, reinvest wisely, and maintain a balanced lifestyle. Others, driven by beliefs equating money with freedom from restraint, overspend, over-leverage, and ultimately collapse into financial ruin. The difference is not the market, the opportunity, or even luck, but the set of habits and assumptions carried into the moment of success. The contradiction lies in how similar levels of income can produce radically different results depending on the architecture of the money mind.

These case studies also illuminate the psychological weight of cultural expectations. The surgeon's financial precarity is not simply a matter of personal weakness but of professional culture. High-status professions are accompanied by powerful social scripts about how one should live. Colleagues live in certain postcodes, drive particular cars, and enrol children in elite schools. Deviating from these norms feels like social demotion, even if it would produce greater financial security. The teacher, by contrast, may inhabit a professional culture where modest living is expected, even respected. The absence of pressure to display wealth allows more freedom to pursue stability. Thus, it is not merely individual psychology but also cultural context that amplifies or alleviates financial stress.

Philosophically, these contradictions challenge the deeply ingrained belief that income is the master key to wellbeing. If income truly dictated destiny, the financial lives of high earners would be predictably secure, and those of modest earners predictably fragile. Reality defies this logic. The evidence points instead to a subtler truth: that money serves as a mirror, reflecting back the beliefs and behaviours of the person holding it. For the prudent, it compounds stability; for the reckless, it magnifies instability. Income enlarges possibility, but it does not determine outcome.

Recognising this has profound implications. It means that the pursuit of higher income, while not unimportant, is insufficient as a strategy for security. Without reshaping the habits and beliefs of the money mind, more income merely amplifies existing patterns. A spender with £40,000 becomes a spender with £200,000; the scale of purchases changes, but the insecurity remains. A saver with £30,000 becomes a saver with £60,000; the capacity grows, but the orientation endures. In both cases, the inner script dictates the outer reality.

These contradictions matter because they cut against the cultural grain. We are conditioned to see salary as the ultimate indicator of financial wellbeing, and to structure life choices around maximising income. Parents, teachers, and policymakers often frame career guidance around earnings potential as though financial security were guaranteed by paycheques alone. Yet case after case reveals that what determines security is not merely earning power but the discipline, perspective, and emotional relationship to money that accompany it. By bringing these contradictions into view, we confront the gap between cultural myth and lived truth.

Ultimately, the stories of the wealthy teacher and indebted surgeon are not anecdotes meant to entertain but signposts to a larger reality. They illustrate that money outcomes are the product of deep, often invisible variables: habits built over decades, emotions tied to self-worth, and beliefs absorbed from family and culture. These elements form the money mind, the hidden force that explains why some thrive while others falter under identical or even superior circumstances. Recognising this shifts the question from "How much do I earn?" to "What is the script guiding my behaviour with what I earn?" It is in this recognition that the possibility of lasting change begins.

Chapter 2
Inherited Scripts

Few aspects of money are as underestimated as the influence of childhood. Long before we earn our first salary, apply for credit, or make conscious choices about saving and spending, we are absorbing lessons that will shape our relationship with money for decades. These lessons are rarely presented as formal teachings. Instead, they are woven into the background of daily life: the tone of voice when parents say "we can't afford that," the tension that hovers around the kitchen table when bills are due, the exhilaration of watching money spent with abandon, or the quiet security that comes from observing a parent put something aside each month. These early impressions form what psychologists call "money scripts"—internalised beliefs about money that operate largely beneath awareness, guiding adult decisions long after the childhood context has faded.

Money scripts are powerful because they bypass logic. They do not present themselves as opinions that can be debated but as assumptions that feel self-evident. A child raised in scarcity may internalise the belief that resources are perpetually at risk of running out. This belief can manifest in adulthood as relentless over-saving, where financial prudence hardens into compulsion, or paradoxically as compulsive spending, where money is treated as fleeting and must be enjoyed before it disappears. Similarly, children who grow up with financial abundance may inherit the message that money is always available, that risk carries little consequence, or that consumption is a form of entitlement. The same circumstances can yield different expressions depending on temperament and context, but the underlying commonality is that *early exposure shapes the internal map.* Adults navigating financial choices are rarely operating with a blank slate; they are acting on scripts written years earlier, often without conscious consent.

The influence of parents is especially complex because much of it is conveyed without direct instruction. Some parents avoid talking about money altogether, believing that silence protects children from worry. Yet silence itself communicates: it can imply that money is taboo, too shameful or frightening to discuss. Others inadvertently pass on their anxieties through visible behaviours—snapping at one another during bill-paying, obsessing over bargains, or expressing guilt when buying something for themselves. Generosity, too, is observed and absorbed. A parent who gives freely, whether of money, time, or resources, signals that money is not merely a means of survival but a medium of connection. These subtler influences can be more enduring than any deliberate advice. Children watch, internalise, and replay these attitudes as adults, often without realising they are acting out inherited scripts rather than consciously chosen beliefs.

Research confirms the durability of these patterns. Studies in financial psychology show that adults' attitudes towards saving, spending, and debt correlate strongly with the messages they absorbed in childhood. A 2011 study by Brad Klontz and colleagues, for instance, identified distinct categories of money scripts—such as "money avoidance," "money worship," "money status," and "money vigilance"—that emerge from early experiences and continue to shape behaviour. Those who grew up in households where money was a source of conflict were more likely to develop avoidance behaviours, shunning financial planning or delaying engagement with money altogether. Those raised with messages equating money and worth were more likely to adopt status-driven spending patterns. What emerges is a picture of continuity: our present financial lives often echo our childhood environments more than we care to admit.

The cultural ideal of meritocracy suggests that financial outcomes are the result of individual effort and intelligence. Yet the concept of inherited scripts complicates this narrative. A child raised in a household of financial fear may carry a constant undertone of anxiety, regardless of their actual earnings as an adult. They may find it difficult to enjoy money, to invest with confidence, or to take calculated risks. Conversely, a child raised in an environment where money was treated with calm and clarity may approach financial decisions with greater resilience, even if their income is modest. The inheritance of attitude, in many cases, proves more decisive than the inheritance of wealth. It is not uncommon for individuals who receive financial windfalls—through inheritance, settlements, or sudden income surges—to squander them quickly if their underlying scripts are disordered. The money comes, but the mind is unprepared to manage it.

This invisible inheritance is perhaps more consequential than the tangible assets passed down between generations. Money can be spent, lost, or redistributed; beliefs endure. Families that never accumulate wealth may nonetheless transmit patterns of frugality, perseverance, and collective support that enable children to build security in adulthood. Families with abundant resources may inadvertently instil recklessness, entitlement, or avoidance, leading descendants to squander advantages. In both cases, the true legacy is not measured in the currency of assets but in the currency of scripts.

Modern examples abound. Financial counsellors often encounter clients who, despite high incomes, remain mired in destructive cycles. One executive earning a substantial salary confessed that he could not save a penny because he grew up watching his parents spend everything as soon as it came in, always fearful that tomorrow would take it away. The pattern of living "for today" was so ingrained that saving felt pointless, almost unnatural. Another client, raised in a household where every purchase was scrutinised and money was associated with guilt, struggled to enjoy even modest spending as an adult. She accumulated significant savings but lived in perpetual fear of running out, depriving herself of comfort or joy. In both cases, the clients were not consciously choosing these behaviours; they were replaying inherited scripts.

The importance of inherited scripts becomes even clearer when viewed across generations. A child raised in a household defined by scarcity may raise their own children in an environment of excess as an overcorrection, determined not to replicate the anxieties of their youth. Yet this can create new problems, instilling in the next generation an unrealistic sense of entitlement or detachment from financial reality. Conversely, a parent who grew up in excess may become hyper-vigilant, overemphasising discipline and self-denial, transmitting scarcity even where abundance exists. Thus, financial scripts are not only inherited but often distorted through cycles of compensation. What begins as one generation's adaptation to circumstance can become the next generation's burden.

Understanding inherited scripts requires honesty and reflection. It demands that we examine not just what we believe about money, but where those beliefs originated. Did we learn to equate money with safety, love, or status? Did we absorb silence as a sign that money is dangerous to discuss? Did we inherit the conviction that no matter how much we have, it will never be enough? These questions are not academic exercises; they are the first steps in recognising how the past continues to shape the present. Awareness does not erase scripts, but it loosens their grip, allowing us to consider whether the lessons we absorbed are still relevant or whether they perpetuate harm.

This chapter is an invitation to interrogate that inheritance. By examining money stories from childhood, the roles of scarcity, fear, and excess, the subtle power of parental influence, and the ways invisible inheritances transmit across generations, we can begin to see our financial behaviours in a new light. What emerges is a recognition that our financial present is never entirely self-authored; it is built upon the scaffolding of earlier scripts. Yet this recognition also opens the door to agency. Scripts can be acknowledged, challenged, and rewritten. The past need not dictate the future. What we inherit does not define what we must pass on. The power lies in choosing which lessons to continue and which to leave behind.

Money Stories from Childhood

By the time most people open their first bank account, much of their financial psychology is already in place. The scripts that govern how they save, spend, borrow, and give are not consciously chosen but shaped long before adulthood, during the formative years of childhood. These money stories—impressions gathered not from formal lessons but from daily exposure to how parents and caregivers behave around money—become mental models that quietly guide decision-making for decades. They are not simply memories of specific events but enduring frameworks through which the adult self interprets financial choices. What makes them so powerful is that they are absorbed without scrutiny, becoming part of the background of identity in the same way that language or cultural norms are.

A child who grows up hearing "we can't afford that" is not merely learning about the limitations of the household budget. They are absorbing an implicit belief about scarcity—that desires and needs are constantly constrained by lack. Over time, this message may evolve into an adult conviction that there is never enough, no matter how much is earned or saved. This person might become an over-saver, hoarding resources as protection against imagined crises, unable to feel secure even with ample reserves. Alternatively, the same early script can manifest in compulsive spending, driven by the unconscious sense that money is fleeting and must be enjoyed before it disappears. The precise behaviour differs, but the underlying narrative—the fear of scarcity—remains intact.

Equally influential are the childhood experiences of witnessing reckless spending. For some, growing up in a household where money was spent impulsively creates a deep resistance to financial risk. These individuals may adopt rigid structures, meticulously track expenses, and avoid debt at all costs. For others, witnessing reckless spending normalises it, making extravagance or short-term gratification feel like a natural rhythm of life. In both cases, the behaviour is not driven primarily by conscious reasoning but by the internalised story of how money "ought" to be handled, absorbed before the child had the maturity to question or contextualise it.

The complexity deepens when we consider that money scripts are not formed solely from what is said but also from what is left unsaid. Silence itself communicates meaning. Parents who never discuss money in front of their children may believe they are shielding them from worry, yet the absence of dialogue often sends the message that money is either taboo or dangerous to talk about. A child raised in such an environment may grow into an adult who avoids financial conversations altogether, reluctant to negotiate salaries, fearful of discussing debt, or hesitant to seek advice. Avoidance becomes a learned behaviour, transmitted not through explicit instruction but through omission.

The emotional tone surrounding money in a household is often more influential than the numbers involved. A family living on modest means but treating money with calm, openness, and mutual respect may raise children who view money as a manageable part of life. A wealthier family where money is accompanied by tension, secrecy, or guilt may raise children who associate financial matters with stress and shame. What matters most is not the amount of money present but the *emotional climate* in which it is managed. Adults frequently find themselves reliving those climates: feeling guilt when spending on themselves, anxiety when bills arrive, or compulsion to buy gifts as proof of love.

Cross-cultural research illustrates the depth of these effects. In societies where collective survival is emphasised, children often grow up equating money with obligation—to family, to community, to group stability. In highly individualistic societies, children may absorb messages equating money with independence or personal achievement. These cultural backdrops shape money stories alongside family influences, embedding values that may persist even when individuals consciously reject them. For example, an adult who intellectually embraces minimalism may still feel compelled to accumulate wealth as proof of worth if raised in a culture that idolises financial success.

Real-world cases highlight how pervasive these scripts can be. A successful professional in their forties, earning a generous salary, might still struggle with the sense that they are "one step away from disaster" because their parents frequently reminded them of the family's precarious finances. Despite evidence of stability, the adult cannot shake the underlying belief that collapse is imminent. Another individual raised in a household where spending was used as emotional balm may continue the pattern, reaching for purchases whenever stress arises. Even when debt accumulates, the behaviour feels almost automatic, tied less to conscious choice than to early associations between spending and relief. These examples illustrate how money stories from childhood persist beneath awareness, resurfacing in ways that defy logic but align with early conditioning.

One of the most striking aspects of money stories is their longevity. Many people inherit not only the lessons of their parents but also the legacies of grandparents and earlier generations, carried through repeated patterns of speech and behaviour. A grandmother who endured wartime scarcity may instil in her children the urgency of frugality, which is then passed on, perhaps unconsciously, to grandchildren. These descendants may feel an ingrained need to conserve, even when they have never personally experienced deprivation. What began as an adaptive response to genuine hardship becomes a script played out in entirely different contexts. This is what makes money stories both powerful and problematic: they are forged in specific historical or familial circumstances but survive long after those circumstances have changed.

It is tempting to think of childhood money stories as fixed determinants of adult behaviour, but they are better understood as invisible scaffolding—structures that shape choices but can be remodelled once recognised. The difficulty lies in surfacing them. Because they were absorbed so early, many adults do not realise their financial behaviours are echoes of childhood scripts. They may interpret compulsive saving as rational caution or overspending as personal weakness, without connecting these tendencies to the stories they inherited. Reflection—sometimes prompted by therapy, coaching, or financial crises—reveals the lineage of these behaviours. Once acknowledged, scripts can be interrogated: does this belief still serve me? Is it aligned with my current reality, or is it a relic of someone else's circumstances?

Understanding money stories from childhood provides a critical foundation for reshaping the money mind. They are the original architecture upon which later habits, decisions, and rationalisations are built. Recognising their influence allows us to distinguish between what is authentically ours and what has been unconsciously inherited. It also helps dismantle shame. Realising that destructive behaviours are not simply personal failings but the continuation of early conditioning creates space for compassion and change. The stories we absorbed without choice can be rewritten with awareness, allowing us to author new scripts that reflect not the fears or excesses of the past but the realities and aspirations of the present.

Every adult carries money stories from childhood, whether they are aware of them or not. These stories shape the way we view scarcity and abundance, the way we respond to stress and opportunity, and the way we define security and success. They influence the careers we choose, the risks we take, and the relationships we form. To ignore them is to risk living on autopilot, guided by scripts that may no longer make sense. To examine them is to take the first step toward genuine financial agency.

Scarcity, Fear, and Excess

The earliest experiences of money are never neutral. They are charged with emotion, shaped by the environments in which children grow up, and carried forward into adult life in ways that often bypass conscious reflection. Scarcity, fear, and excess each leave distinct imprints, creating money behaviours that may appear contradictory but share a common thread: they originate not in present-day circumstances but in the psychological residue of childhood. What begins as an adaptation to a particular environment becomes an enduring script, replayed decades later in contexts where it no longer makes sense.

Scarcity is perhaps the most obvious and the most enduring of these imprints. A child who grows up with limited resources learns quickly that money is fragile and that every choice carries weight. Meals may be stretched, bills deferred, and desires postponed indefinitely. These children internalise the message that life is precarious and that financial security can never be taken for granted. As adults, they often carry this scarcity mindset even when their material conditions have changed. For some, this manifests as relentless over-saving. They accumulate money compulsively, not for enjoyment but as a bulwark against imagined disaster. Even in periods of stability, they cannot relax, convinced that collapse is just around the corner. The paradox is that their financial habits achieve the very security they craved as children, yet they rarely experience the psychological relief that security should bring. *The fear of scarcity survives long after the scarcity itself has ended.*

For others, childhood deprivation produces the opposite behaviour. The memory of going without makes them determined never to feel that sense of lack again. They spend impulsively, seizing opportunities for pleasure or status as if tomorrow will rob them of the chance. In this pattern, money is treated as transient, something to be enjoyed before it inevitably disappears. Both compulsive saving and compulsive spending emerge from the same root: an early encounter with scarcity that made money feel volatile and uncertain. The divergence lies in whether the adult self responds by hoarding against the future or grasping at the present. In both cases, the past dictates the present, even when circumstances no longer justify such extremes.

Fear compounds the effects of scarcity but can also arise in households where money was present but unstable. Children may witness parents arguing about bills, debts, or unwise financial decisions, and from this they internalise not only the idea that money is limited but that it is dangerous. Money becomes synonymous with conflict, shame, or insecurity. Adults shaped by these experiences often struggle to approach financial matters calmly. They may avoid looking at bank statements, procrastinate on tax returns, or resist budgeting because doing so triggers the same anxiety they felt in childhood. In other cases, they overcompensate, seeking control through meticulous accounting or rigid discipline, attempting to master the fear by containing it. What unites these responses is that money is not experienced as neutral; it is imbued with emotional weight, and the fear attached to it continues to dictate behaviour long after the original circumstances are gone.

Excess, on the other hand, produces a different but equally distorting set of scripts. A child who grows up in abundance may never learn the practical limits of money. When every request is met with immediate fulfilment, when toys, clothes, or experiences arrive without delay or explanation, the implicit message is that money is inexhaustible. In adulthood, this can translate into entitlement—an expectation that resources will always be available, that lifestyles can be maintained without effort, and that financial consequences are unlikely to apply personally. The danger here is not ignorance of financial principles but indifference to them. These individuals may spend freely, take on debt with little hesitation, or approach investment with undue risk, assuming that resources will replenish themselves.

Yet excess can also lead to avoidance. Some children raised in wealth are so conscious of its presence that they recoil from it. They may have observed parents using money as a tool of control, status, or performance, and conclude that engagement with money is morally tainted. As adults, they may underplay their financial privileges, avoid conversations about money, or resist engaging with their wealth altogether. This avoidance does not prevent financial outcomes, but it does leave them ill-prepared to manage resources responsibly. In both entitlement and avoidance, the underlying dynamic is the same: excess distorts the perception of money, either by exaggerating its availability or by making it too fraught to handle directly.

The intergenerational nature of these patterns is striking. Scarcity, fear, and excess do not end with the children who first experience them; they ripple forward. A parent who grew up in deprivation may raise their children with hyper-vigilance, constantly emphasising frugality even when the family is secure. The message transmitted is not stability but anxiety, and the children inherit the fear as much as the discipline. Conversely, a parent who grew up in excess may attempt to shield their children by downplaying wealth or by indulging them uncritically, inadvertently passing on either entitlement or avoidance. What began as an adaptive response in one generation becomes a burden in the next, perpetuating cycles of distorted financial behaviour even in the absence of the original conditions.

Real-world examples illustrate these dynamics vividly. Financial advisers often encounter clients with substantial assets who still feel impoverished. One such client, raised in a household where scarcity dominated every decision, found it impossible to enjoy a comfortable retirement despite a seven-figure portfolio. Their anxiety was not alleviated by financial facts because it was not rooted in the present but in childhood scripts. Conversely, advisers also meet high-income professionals who spend recklessly, unable to build savings despite lucrative careers. Many trace their habits back to childhood environments where money was either abundant or unstable, normalising immediate gratification or avoidance of financial realities. These are not anomalies but patterns, repeated across social and economic contexts, reminding us that *money behaviour is psychological inheritance as much as personal choice.*

Philosophically, the stories of scarcity, fear, and excess remind us that money is never simply material. It carries meaning, and that meaning is formed early. Scarcity teaches that money is fragile. Fear teaches that money is dangerous. Excess teaches that money is either limitless or corrupting. These lessons, absorbed before critical reflection is possible, continue to operate long after childhood ends. The challenge of adulthood is to recognise which scripts we have inherited and to decide whether they still serve us. Left unexamined, they exert quiet but powerful influence, shaping careers, relationships, and identities. Brought into awareness, they can be questioned, reshaped, and rewritten.

The enduring power of these childhood imprints is that they blur the line between past and present. An adult living with financial security may still act as if disaster looms. Another surrounded by abundance may act as if money will always replenish itself, no matter what. These are not logical responses to present circumstances but echoes of earlier experiences replayed in a different context. By tracing behaviours back to the scripts of scarcity, fear, and excess, we gain not only insight but the possibility of change. Recognition is the first act of freedom: the ability to distinguish between what belongs to the past and what belongs to the present, and to choose consciously rather than repeat unconsciously.

Scarcity, fear, and excess shape financial behaviour not because they dictate outcomes mechanically, but because they create the psychological frameworks through which choices are interpreted. They are the invisible architecture beneath the visible numbers. To understand them is to understand why intelligent, capable adults so often make decisions that seem illogical from the outside but perfectly consistent from within the logic of their inherited scripts. It is to see that money is not just currency but memory, not just transaction but transmission. And it is to acknowledge that the path to financial health lies not merely in changing numbers on a page, but in rewriting the stories carried forward from childhood.

Parental Influence Without Words

Children learn about money long before they can count it. The lessons are not delivered through lectures or worksheets but through observation—tone of voice, body language, and the emotional atmosphere surrounding financial events. Parents transmit powerful beliefs about money not only in what they say, but in what they do not say. Silence, stress, generosity, avoidance, and ritual all become part of the unspoken curriculum. These subtle forms of communication often shape financial attitudes more enduringly than explicit advice, precisely because they are absorbed unconsciously and without resistance.

Consider the recurring scene of bill-paying in many households. A parent sits at the kitchen table with a stack of envelopes, brows furrowed, sighs escaping. The child may not know the details—mortgage rates, utility charges, or minimum payments—but they learn quickly that money is accompanied by tension. They internalise the message that financial management is stressful, burdensome, even fearful. Years later, as adults, they may procrastinate on their own bills, avoid budgeting software, or feel a wave of anxiety whenever they check their account balance. The child's early association between money and distress becomes the adult's reflexive response, even in very different circumstances. *The silence of figures on the page is replaced by the loudness of the emotions once attached to them.*

Equally powerful is the lesson of silence itself. In many families, money is simply not discussed. Children may never hear their parents talk openly about earnings, savings, or financial priorities. The absence of dialogue communicates its own meaning: that money is private, taboo, or unsafe to bring up. Adults raised in such households often replicate the avoidance. They shy away from conversations about salary, negotiate less assertively, or struggle to discuss financial planning with partners. The lack of words in childhood becomes the absence of language in adulthood, leaving people unequipped to articulate their needs or navigate financial decisions collaboratively. Silence, in this sense, is not neutrality—it is instruction.

Then there are households where generosity is visible and consistent. A parent who habitually gives to neighbours, supports community causes, or helps relatives in need transmits a belief that money is not only for individual security but also for shared wellbeing. The child raised in such an environment may develop a lasting orientation toward generosity, treating money as a means of connection rather than solely as protection. Yet even here the lessons are layered: if generosity is performed with joy, it communicates abundance and trust. If given grudgingly or accompanied by resentment, it may teach the child that giving is obligation rather than choice, creating conflicted attitudes in adulthood. The nuance lies not in the act itself but in the emotional context in which it is carried out.

Parental influence without words also operates through daily micro-behaviours. A parent who insists on paying in cash, for example, may unintentionally communicate suspicion of credit or digital banking, leading their children to inherit a mistrust of financial technology. A parent who casually overspends on holidays but becomes visibly stressed when the credit card bill arrives teaches both indulgence and guilt, a contradictory pairing that often surfaces in adults who oscillate between spending sprees and self-recrimination. A parent who celebrates each pay day with a family outing may instil the idea that income is to be enjoyed immediately rather than allocated prudently. These are not deliberate teachings, but children do not need explanations to learn; they absorb meaning from pattern and repetition.

The impact of these unspoken lessons has been documented in behavioural research. Studies show that financial behaviours are often transmitted intergenerationally, even when children reject or criticise their parents' approaches. For example, adults who grew up in households where money was a source of conflict are more likely to experience financial arguments in their own relationships, even if they consciously vow to avoid repeating their parents' mistakes. The reason is that *emotional templates are more enduring than intellectual intentions*. People revert to the patterns they witnessed because those patterns defined what felt "normal."

There is also a cultural dimension to these influences. In some societies, parents avoid discussing money not out of secrecy but out of propriety; financial matters are considered private and impolite to raise. In others, parents openly discuss budgets and priorities, inviting children into the process as a way of modelling responsibility. These cultural norms intersect with individual family practices to produce a complex inheritance. A child raised in a culture of openness but a family of silence, or vice versa, may grow up with conflicted money attitudes, oscillating between disclosure and secrecy depending on context. The interplay of personal and cultural silence amplifies or mitigates the strength of the inherited script.

The subtlety of non-verbal parental influence can also make it resistant to change. Explicit lessons can be questioned or reinterpreted—an adult can remember being told "money doesn't grow on trees" and decide whether they agree. But the quiet signals absorbed from body language, tone, or omission rarely surface to consciousness. People often enact these scripts without realising where they came from. A woman may discover, only in therapy or financial coaching, that her avoidance of financial discussions with her partner mirrors the silence she grew up with. A man may realise that his need to give extravagantly at holidays is not generosity freely chosen but an imitation of his father's ritual of overcompensating for absences. Recognition often comes late because the influence was never named to begin with.

It is tempting to assume that children learn primarily through what parents say, but in financial matters the reverse is often true: the most lasting lessons are communicated indirectly. Children learn not only from the explicit "yes" or "no" but from the sigh, the silence, the argument, the gift, the avoidance, the ritual. These influences shape whether money feels like a source of anxiety or agency, whether it is treated as a private burden or a shared resource, whether it carries shame or possibility. By recognising the weight of what is unspoken, we begin to understand why financial behaviours are so persistent and why they often resist rational explanation.

Parental influence without words demonstrates that money is never merely material. It is emotional, social, and symbolic, and children internalise these dimensions through observation long before they manage money themselves. For adults seeking to rewrite their money mind, uncovering these silent inheritances is crucial. The stress at bill time, the silence around earnings, the joy or resentment in generosity—these form the foundations of financial psychology. To see them clearly is to gain the power to choose differently, to replace inherited silence with dialogue, inherited stress with clarity, and inherited guilt with intentionality.

The Invisible Inheritance

When most people think of inheritance, they imagine property deeds, trust funds, or family heirlooms. Yet the most influential legacies rarely arrive in the form of cheques or legal documents. They come instead as ingrained assumptions, emotional reflexes, and unspoken scripts that shape financial behaviour across generations. These invisible inheritances—beliefs about scarcity, entitlement, risk, generosity, and worth—often prove more powerful than material wealth. Money itself can be lost, spent, or redistributed. Scripts endure, dictating how money is perceived and managed long after the original inheritance is gone.

The distinction becomes clear when comparing families with similar financial circumstances but radically different outcomes. Two siblings may each receive a modest inheritance of £20,000 from their parents. One treats it as a foundation, investing cautiously, augmenting it with consistent saving, and ultimately building financial stability. The other, carrying a script that money is fleeting and meant to be spent quickly, dissipates the funds within months on short-lived indulgences. The disparity is not explained by the size of the inheritance, which is identical, but by the beliefs that accompanied it. *The invisible inheritance defines what the tangible inheritance becomes.*

This phenomenon is not limited to modest sums. Studies of lottery winners reveal that many return to financial difficulty within a few years of their windfall. Despite the sudden influx of wealth, their underlying scripts remain unchanged. If they have always equated money with self-worth, they spend conspicuously to signal status. If they have always felt unsafe financially, they hoard excessively but without strategy, often leaving themselves illiquid and anxious. In contrast, individuals who inherit constructive scripts—such as the value of delayed gratification or the discipline of budgeting—can preserve and grow resources even when the amounts are modest. The durability of invisible inheritance makes it more decisive than the visible one.

Consider also the paradox of families with intergenerational wealth who nonetheless experience repeated financial collapse. Case studies from family business research reveal that wealth rarely survives beyond the third generation. The first generation builds it, the second maintains it, and the third often squanders it. The reason is not simply extravagance but the erosion of financial scripts. The founding generation typically operates with a scarcity mindset, rooted in the struggle of creation. The second generation, observing both scarcity and success, balances caution with opportunity. The third generation, shielded from the original struggle, may inherit abundance but not the attitudes that sustained it. Entitlement replaces vigilance, avoidance replaces discipline, and the wealth unravels. The visible inheritance cannot compensate for the absence of the invisible one.

The transmission of these hidden scripts often occurs through subtle, everyday experiences. A child who observes a parent refusing to discuss money may inherit not just ignorance but avoidance, treating financial matters as shameful or overwhelming. Another who witnesses parents giving generously, even in lean times, may internalise the belief that money is a tool for connection and purpose. These inheritances require no explicit instruction; they are absorbed through observation and repetition. Adults often enact them without awareness, believing their financial behaviours are self-directed when they are in fact echoes of earlier generations.

Invisible inheritance also explains why financial struggles recur across family lines, even when income levels differ dramatically. A parent who lived through economic instability may pass down an anxious script of "never enough," instilling in their children an inability to feel secure regardless of earnings. These children may grow into high-income professionals yet remain driven by the same fear of loss, overworking and underspending in a pattern that perpetuates insecurity. Conversely, a family accustomed to treating money as inexhaustible may raise children who replicate that assumption, regardless of whether their own incomes support it. What appears from the outside as puzzling behaviour—over-saving in abundance or overspending in scarcity—is perfectly consistent when understood as continuity of inherited scripts.

The potency of these scripts lies in their invisibility. Material inheritance can be counted and allocated; financial habits passed down silently resist measurement. Most people can recall the size of a parental bequest but struggle to articulate the beliefs about money they inherited. The invisibility makes them harder to interrogate, yet also more pervasive. They shape not just how money is spent or saved but how it is felt—whether it is a source of anxiety, security, identity, or shame. As a result, they infiltrate not only financial decisions but also career choices, relationship dynamics, and self-concept.

The philosophical weight of invisible inheritance lies in its challenge to common assumptions about financial success. Cultural narratives often frame outcomes as products of either hard work or fortune. Yet the deeper determinant is neither effort nor luck but the scripts carried within. A hardworking individual with destructive scripts may undermine their own progress repeatedly, while a modest earner with constructive scripts may quietly accumulate security. Invisible inheritance reframes wealth not as an external possession but as an internalised orientation. The financial life we live is less a reflection of our present choices than of the unconscious scripts handed down from the past.

Examples of this dynamic are evident across cultures and contexts. Immigrant families often carry forward scripts of scarcity, forged in the struggle of resettlement, even as subsequent generations achieve prosperity. Wealthier families, in contrast, may transmit scripts of abundance or entitlement, leaving descendants ill-prepared for financial shocks. The cultural and historical backdrops change, but the mechanism remains the same: what is transmitted is not only resources but *rules of engagement with resources*. These rules persist even when the circumstances that created them have disappeared.

Recognising the power of invisible inheritance is more than an intellectual exercise. It opens the door to agency. Scripts may be inherited, but they are not immutable. The adult who realises that their compulsion to hoard stems from a grandparent's scarcity script can begin to question whether the behaviour aligns with their current reality. The professional who identifies that their avoidance of financial planning is a repetition of their parents' silence can choose to break the pattern by engaging deliberately with money. The invisible inheritance may explain behaviour, but awareness is the first step to rewriting it.

Ultimately, invisible inheritance underscores a simple but profound truth: the most decisive legacies are not the ones written in wills but the ones etched in behaviour. Families may pass down wealth, but more often they pass down attitudes that determine whether wealth is preserved, squandered, or created anew. The true inheritance is not the money itself but the money mind. To understand this is to recognise that financial wellbeing is less about what is given and more about what is taught—consciously or not—across generations.

Chapter 3
The Emotional Economy

Money is often presented as the domain of logic, arithmetic, and spreadsheets. Yet anyone who has ever bought something they could not afford, delayed paying a bill out of dread, or splurged in a moment of loneliness knows that financial life is rarely rational. Beneath the surface of every balance sheet lies a current of emotions that drives behaviour more powerfully than mathematics ever could. Purchases that appear practical are often emotional transactions in disguise: the comforting meal after a stressful day, the new outfit that promises a fleeting sense of identity, the holiday booked less for rest than for validation. Numbers may record the outcome, but the underlying engine is emotional need. To understand money as emotion rather than mathematics is to acknowledge that financial decisions are rarely about the price tag alone; they are about the invisible triggers of stress, boredom, insecurity, and desire that turn transactions into coping strategies.

The emotional pull of money becomes clear when observing the way financial choices are entangled with self-image. A person does not simply buy clothes; they buy a signal of who they are, or who they want to be. A car is rarely just transport—it is mobility combined with identity, an external declaration of belonging or aspiration. Even mundane items carry emotional freight: the brand of coffee chosen, the phone upgraded, the gift selected for a friend. Each decision contains layers of meaning about comfort, validation, or connection. Economists may speak of utility, but in daily life, utility is filtered through emotional resonance. This is why a decision that looks irrational to one observer—overspending on designer trainers or pouring money into hobbies—can feel perfectly rational to the individual, because it meets an unacknowledged emotional demand.

Yet emotions not only motivate purchases; they also shape the aftermath of financial decisions. When those choices lead to mistakes—missed payments, mounting debt, or spending regret—the emotional response is often far more severe than the financial consequence itself. Money mistakes carry a particular kind of shame, one that can feel heavier than mistakes in other areas of life. People will speak openly about health problems or failed relationships but remain silent about debt or financial mismanagement, even with close friends. This silence reinforces secrecy, and secrecy deepens the problem. Instead of seeking support or advice, individuals avoid confronting their finances, hoping the issue will recede, all while anxiety mounts. The shame attached to financial failure is so disproportionate that it often locks people into destructive cycles. What could be addressed through transparency becomes entrenched through avoidance.

Spending also functions as a form of self-expression, a way of shaping identity in a world where identity itself feels increasingly precarious. In modern consumer societies, people are constantly encouraged to define themselves by what they buy—what brands they wear, what experiences they share online, what lifestyle markers they display. For some, spending becomes a way to belong, to signal membership in a group or alignment with a trend. For others, it becomes a way to assert individuality, to stand apart by curating distinctive tastes. In both cases, the act of purchase carries meaning beyond the item itself. It is communication, often unconscious, about who we think we are or who we want others to believe we are. The paradox is that this form of self-expression can deepen dependence on external validation, making identity contingent on consumption rather than internal coherence.

Debt reveals the emotional undercurrents most starkly. While debt is commonly discussed in terms of interest rates and repayment schedules, it often functions as something deeper: a form of emotional armour. People take on debt not merely to access goods but to shield themselves from insecurity, to maintain appearances, or to avoid confronting deeper anxieties. A professional who feels inadequate compared to peers may finance a lifestyle through credit to project success. A parent who cannot bear the thought of their child "going without" may overextend financially to preserve a sense of adequacy. In each case, the debt is not simply financial—it is protective, a way of managing the emotions that come with vulnerability. Yet the protection is temporary, and the armour soon becomes a prison, adding anxiety to the very insecurities it was meant to conceal.

The emotional economy is therefore not a marginal aspect of financial life; it is its central logic. Numbers matter, but they are never neutral. They are filtered through the emotional landscapes of fear, pride, longing, shame, and hope. To grasp this is to recognise why financial advice that addresses only calculation so often fails. Telling someone to "spend less than they earn" or to "pay down debt aggressively" may be mathematically sound, but it ignores the emotional drivers that made overspending or borrowing feel necessary in the first place. Real change requires engaging with the emotions beneath the numbers, surfacing the triggers, and reshaping the scripts.

This chapter turns directly to those forces. It examines how purchases serve emotional needs more than practical ones, how shame and secrecy distort financial behaviour, how spending functions as self-expression, and how debt operates as armour. Together, these insights reveal that financial life cannot be understood through arithmetic alone. It must be approached as an emotional ecosystem, one where feelings often precede figures. Recognising this reality is not an indulgence but a necessity. Only by acknowledging the emotional dimension of money can individuals hope to rewrite the patterns that undermine them, replacing reflex with awareness and anxiety with agency. The economy that matters most is not external but internal: the economy of emotions that governs the way money is used, avoided, or feared.

Money as Emotion, Not Math

Few forces in life are treated as more rational than money. From the earliest lessons in arithmetic, children are told that financial decisions are about addition and subtraction, costs and benefits, assets and liabilities. Yet the lived reality of money exposes a different truth: purchases and financial choices are rarely cold calculations. They are instead deeply emotional acts, saturated with meaning and bound to human needs for comfort, identity, and validation. What appears to be a transaction for goods or services is often a transaction for feelings—an attempt to soothe stress, quell loneliness, reward effort, or affirm belonging. To reduce money to mathematics is to ignore its role as one of the most potent emotional currencies in human life.

One of the clearest indicators that money is emotional rather than purely rational is the phenomenon of retail therapy. Countless people turn to shopping not because they need a particular item but because they are stressed, anxious, or fatigued. The act of buying provides a momentary release, a sense of control in an otherwise chaotic day. Psychologists describe this as *affect regulation*—the use of external actions to stabilise internal states. For a stressed professional, ordering a meal delivery may not simply provide food but reassurance that they can treat themselves. For a student feeling overwhelmed, purchasing clothes online might be less about fashion and more about reclaiming a sense of agency. The expenditure is a strategy for emotional management disguised as consumption. From a mathematical perspective, it is illogical; from an emotional perspective, it is perfectly consistent.

Loneliness provides another trigger for emotionally driven spending. The individual who dines out frequently not for the food but for the social setting, or who invests in experiences they can post online, may be seeking connection as much as consumption. The modern economy capitalises on this dynamic: companies sell not only products but also belonging. A gym membership promises not just fitness but community; a concert ticket offers not only music but shared identity; even a brand of trainers signals association with a tribe. Spending becomes an attempt to bridge emotional gaps, to substitute for intimacy, or to communicate affiliation when words or relationships fall short. The result is that money circulates not only as currency for goods but as currency for connection.

Boredom, too, plays a significant role in consumption patterns. Digital shopping platforms have transformed financial behaviour by making purchases instantaneous and available as a response to idle moments. Browsing online shops during a commute or at night on a phone is less about need and more about stimulation. The purchase provides novelty, anticipation, and the small thrill of reward. Behavioural economists call this the *dopamine effect*—the brain's reward system responding not to possession but to the anticipation of it. The maths of such purchases is often negligible; the emotional impact, however, is powerful. What appears as frivolous spending can be understood as a coping mechanism for emotional stagnation.

Identity forms perhaps the deepest emotional layer of financial behaviour. Every purchase carries a symbolic message: "This is who I am" or "This is who I want to be seen as." A person who buys organic food is rarely paying solely for nutrition; they are paying for an identity that signals health-consciousness, sustainability, or middle-class virtue. A teenager who saves for branded trainers is investing not in footwear but in social legitimacy among peers. Even career professionals who purchase status symbols—luxury watches, high-end cars—are often reinforcing their self-concept or performing a narrative of success. This is why financial decisions are so emotionally charged: they do not only meet practical needs but also shape self-perception. To spend is to construct an identity, and to withhold spending can feel like erasing it.

Validation sits alongside identity as another key emotional driver of money. When individuals spend, they often seek affirmation—either from themselves or from others. A new phone may represent the validation of being technologically current. A generous gift may validate one's role as a caring friend. A holiday may serve to validate success through the performance of leisure. This emotional undercurrent helps explain why people so often exceed budgets for weddings, birthdays, or holidays: these events are laden with social validation, and spending feels inseparable from recognition. The money itself is not the end; it is the vehicle through which people hope to receive affirmation that they matter, that they belong, that they have achieved.

The emotional role of money becomes even clearer when individuals resist or reject spending. Someone who refuses to buy new clothes, who cuts every discretionary expense, may not be operating from pure logic but from fear—fear of loss, fear of scarcity, fear rooted in earlier experiences. Their restraint is emotional as much as the spender's indulgence is. In both directions, money reflects internal states rather than neutral calculations. This is why two individuals with identical incomes and expenses can live radically different financial lives: one feeling constant anxiety, the other feeling ease. The maths may be the same; the emotions are not.

Case studies underline this truth vividly. Take the example of a middle-aged professional earning a comfortable salary who nonetheless feels compelled to shop online nightly. Financially, they can afford the purchases, but emotionally, the act of buying soothes loneliness after their children leave for university. Or consider a young entrepreneur who pours money into luxury experiences to project an image of success to peers, even as their business remains unstable. These choices are not "irrational" in the abstract; they are emotionally rational, aligning with needs that the individuals may not consciously articulate. The fact that the behaviour undermines long-term security does not negate its emotional coherence.

The implication is that traditional financial advice often fails because it ignores the emotional drivers beneath the numbers. Telling someone to "cut unnecessary expenses" or "budget carefully" assumes that purchases are unnecessary in a functional sense. Yet for the spender, they may feel deeply necessary emotionally. Without addressing the stress, loneliness, boredom, or need for identity and validation that drive the spending, the advice is incomplete. This is why so many people, even with financial literacy, struggle to change behaviour: the advice addresses the symptom but not the cause. *The numbers are logical, but the behaviour is emotional.*

Understanding money as emotion rather than math reshapes how we view both success and failure in financial life. Overspending is not always recklessness; it can be a sign of unmet needs. Frugality is not always discipline; it can be anxiety in disguise. Debt is not always irresponsibility; it can be emotional protection. By reframing financial behaviour in emotional terms, we gain empathy for ourselves and others, and we gain the tools to make change that endures. For an individual, this means asking not only "Can I afford this?" but "What emotion am I buying with this?" For society, it means recognising that consumer culture thrives because it sells feelings as much as products.

Money, then, is not merely a tool for exchange; it is a mirror for the human psyche. Each purchase, each act of saving or borrowing, reflects not just a calculation but a state of being. To understand financial behaviour, one must look not only at the numbers but at the emotions that animate them. The story of money is the story of what we fear, what we long for, and what we hope to prove—both to ourselves and to others. This is why financial wellbeing cannot be secured through numbers alone. It requires an honest reckoning with the emotional economy beneath the mathematical one, a recognition that money is as much about the heart as it is about the head.

Shame and Secrecy

Few experiences provoke such disproportionate feelings of shame as financial missteps. A failed business venture, a maxed-out credit card, or even a bounced cheque often generates emotions far heavier than the objective damage caused. Where other mistakes are framed as learning opportunities, money mistakes are treated as moral failings. To owe, to overspend, to mismanage is often internalised as proof of inadequacy, irresponsibility, or weakness. This unique stigma attached to financial failure drives many people into silence, and that silence frequently magnifies the problem. Shame and secrecy are not incidental by-products of money troubles; they are central forces that shape how those troubles unfold, trapping individuals in cycles of avoidance and concealment that erode both wellbeing and financial stability.

The roots of this shame lie in the way societies have entwined money with identity. To be solvent, secure, or successful financially is often seen as evidence of competence, discipline, and even virtue. Conversely, to stumble is seen not simply as a technical setback but as a personal exposure. This moralisation of money has deep historical roots. In many cultures, thrift and self-sufficiency were framed as civic or religious duties, while debt was condemned as weakness or sin. Such attitudes persist, often unconsciously, shaping how people perceive themselves and others in financial distress. This is why otherwise capable, intelligent professionals—doctors, lawyers, academics—can feel crushed by shame when they struggle with credit card debt. The problem is not the figures alone; it is the symbolic meaning attached to those figures.

Secrecy often emerges as a coping mechanism. Embarrassed by their perceived failure, individuals conceal financial difficulties from partners, family, or friends. Some even hide it from themselves, avoiding account statements, delaying bill payments, or shoving unopened letters into drawers. Avoidance provides short-term relief by postponing confrontation with reality, but it compounds the long-term consequences. Interest accrues, penalties mount, and relationships become strained as partners discover hidden debts or unspoken anxieties. The very act of keeping financial troubles secret increases their weight, adding layers of guilt and mistrust to the original challenge. What began as a practical issue evolves into a relational and psychological one.

The destructive interplay of shame and secrecy is particularly evident in the phenomenon of "financial infidelity." Surveys suggest that a significant proportion of couples conceal purchases, debts, or accounts from one another. The motivations vary—fear of conflict, desire to maintain autonomy, or embarrassment at overspending—but the underlying driver is often shame. Rather than risk judgement, individuals choose concealment. The irony is that secrecy tends to damage trust far more severely than financial missteps themselves. A hidden overdraft can destabilise a relationship not because of the sum owed but because it symbolises dishonesty and fear. Once secrecy is discovered, it becomes harder for couples to work together to resolve the financial issue, perpetuating the cycle.

Research into behavioural finance provides further evidence of this cycle. People experiencing financial shame are less likely to seek professional advice, even when affordable or freely available. They are also less likely to disclose problems to supportive networks. Instead, they retreat into isolation, believing their struggles are unique or shameful. Yet data consistently shows that financial missteps are widespread. Large proportions of populations live with persistent credit card debt, struggle with budgeting, or lack emergency savings. What feels like personal failure is, in fact, a common human experience. The secrecy prevents individuals from realising this, leaving them convinced that their situation is abnormal. *Shame thrives in silence; disclosure often diminishes it.*

The disproportionate shame attached to financial errors also reflects the psychological weight of money as a proxy for self-worth. Many individuals tie their value to their earning capacity, spending habits, or accumulated assets. When these fall short of expectations, shame emerges as a defence mechanism, punishing the self for failing to meet internal or external standards. This dynamic helps explain why someone might feel greater shame over a £1,000 overdraft than over a failing relationship or declining health. The overdraft directly threatens their self-concept as competent, responsible, or independent. The money itself is secondary; the identity is primary.

Cultural narratives amplify this effect by glorifying financial success stories while minimising the ordinary struggles behind them. Social media, advertising, and entertainment industries portray prosperity as evidence of intelligence and discipline, erasing the messy realities of debt, insecurity, or failure. In such an environment, admitting financial difficulty feels doubly humiliating: not only is one failing by personal standards, but one is also deviating from the cultural script of upward mobility and self-sufficiency. The gulf between appearance and reality widens, and secrecy becomes the means to maintain appearances.

It is important to note that secrecy is not always deliberate concealment; sometimes it is unconscious avoidance. People postpone checking their bank balance, neglect to file tax returns, or ignore reminders not because they wish to deceive but because confronting reality feels unbearable. Psychologists call this *avoidance coping*, a short-term strategy to reduce distress that ultimately perpetuates it. The unopened bank statement does not eliminate debt; it magnifies the anxiety of the unknown. The energy spent avoiding reality often exceeds what would be required to face it. Yet the pull of avoidance is strong because shame makes engagement feel threatening.

There are contrasting cultural perspectives worth acknowledging. In some societies, collective discussion of money is more normalised, and individuals may feel less shame in disclosing difficulties. Mutual support networks, community lending circles, or extended family assistance can reduce secrecy by reframing financial struggle as a shared challenge rather than a private disgrace. In more individualistic cultures, however, the emphasis on self-reliance intensifies shame. The belief that one should manage alone makes disclosure feel like failure. This divergence highlights that shame is not an inevitable response to financial difficulty; it is a product of cultural framing as much as personal psychology.

Philosophically, the dynamic of shame and secrecy reveals the paradox at the heart of financial life: money is at once a private matter and a deeply social one. People believe they must keep their financial mistakes hidden, yet those mistakes are shaped by—and have consequences for—social relationships. The secrecy intended to protect relationships often corrodes them; the shame intended to enforce responsibility often disables it. Breaking this paradox requires reframing financial missteps not as moral flaws but as human experiences, susceptible to repair and learning. Until that reframing occurs, shame and secrecy will continue to trap individuals in cycles of silence and suffering.

The lesson is stark but liberating: financial shame does not emerge from the size of the mistake but from the meaning attached to it. To miss a bill or fall into debt is not in itself catastrophic; what makes it corrosive is the secrecy that follows. By bringing financial struggles into the open—whether with partners, advisors, or supportive communities—individuals weaken the grip of shame and regain the capacity to act. A culture that recognises the universality of financial missteps, rather than moralising them, creates space for resilience and change. Until then, the most damaging inheritance of financial mistakes will not be the lost money but the silence surrounding it.

Spending as Self-Expression

Every purchase carries a message, whether intended or not. When people choose clothes, cars, holidays, or even the brand of coffee they drink, they are not only meeting a practical need but also communicating something about who they are, who they aspire to be, and where they see themselves fitting into the social fabric. This signalling function of money is rarely conscious, yet it shapes spending decisions with extraordinary force. Far from being merely utilitarian, consumption is often a form of self-expression—an external language through which individuals convey belonging, individuality, and status. What makes this dynamic compelling, and at times troubling, is that the signals we send through spending are not always deliberate, nor are they necessarily aligned with our deeper values. They are shaped by cultural pressures, peer expectations, and unconscious desires as much as by personal choice.

Consider the phenomenon of fashion. Clothing ostensibly serves the practical purpose of covering and protecting the body, but in practice it functions as one of the most visible arenas for self-expression. The student who spends weeks' worth of savings on a branded pair of trainers is not paying for durability or comfort alone; they are purchasing legitimacy in the eyes of their peers, a badge of belonging to a particular group. The professional who invests in tailored suits or designer handbags is signalling competence, status, and alignment with cultural images of success. Even those who reject mainstream trends—choosing vintage, sustainable, or minimalist clothing—are engaging in self-expression, signalling independence, authenticity, or ethical conviction. The money spent is not on fabric but on identity.

The same is true of technology. A smartphone is, at its core, a communication tool. Yet the model and brand chosen communicate much more than utility. Carrying the latest iPhone is often interpreted as a sign of being modern, successful, or connected. Opting for a lesser-known or deliberately modest brand can signal frugality, independence from trends, or even quiet rebellion against consumer culture. This illustrates a crucial point: *spending decisions are rarely neutral.* Even choices framed as practical or restrained are laden with expressive meaning. In contemporary economies, opting out of certain forms of consumption can be as communicative as opting in.

Spending as self-expression extends beyond possessions to experiences. Holidays, concerts, dining choices, and leisure activities increasingly serve as statements about personal identity. A trip to an eco-lodge is not only about relaxation but also about signalling environmental awareness. Attending a music festival is as much about being seen as it is about enjoying the performance. Posting pictures of brunch at a fashionable café communicates a lifestyle narrative to one's social circle. Sociologists call this "conspicuous consumption," but the concept has expanded in the digital age: consumption is no longer only about displaying wealth but about curating identity in ways that align with cultural scripts of uniqueness, authenticity, or sophistication. The performance of self through spending has become continuous, especially when amplified by social media.

It would be simplistic, however, to frame all expressive spending as superficial or manipulative. On a deeper level, purchases genuinely help individuals explore and affirm their sense of self. A young adult experimenting with different styles, hobbies, or travel destinations is using money to test identities. A retiree investing in gardening tools or art classes may be signalling not status but a shift in personal values towards creativity or tranquillity. In such cases, spending functions as a bridge between inner desires and external expression. The risk emerges when the expression becomes divorced from authenticity—when individuals purchase not to affirm their identity but to mask insecurity or conform to imposed standards. At this point, self-expression through spending can become a form of self-alienation.

The tension between individuality and belonging is central to this phenomenon. People spend to differentiate themselves, but they also spend to fit in. A teenager may purchase clothing to avoid social exclusion; a professional may dine at certain restaurants to network effectively; a family may stretch their budget for a car that aligns with neighbourhood norms. Belonging often demands costly signals, and deviation risks exclusion. Yet the very same individuals may spend in other areas to assert uniqueness—choosing distinctive décor, supporting niche brands, or pursuing unusual hobbies. This duality reflects the paradox of modern identity: the desire to be both part of the group and distinct within it. Money provides the means to negotiate this balance, but it also ties identity to material expression in ways that can prove fragile.

Case studies illustrate the stakes. Consider two colleagues with similar incomes. One directs discretionary spending towards luxury goods, aligning with the corporate culture of visible success. The other channels funds into travel and unique experiences, positioning themselves as worldly and unconventional. Both are spending beyond functional need, yet each is curating an identity narrative through money. The outcomes, however, diverge. The first may feel trapped in cycles of escalating status competition, while the second may face financial strain from prioritising experiences over savings. Neither approach is inherently irrational, but both reveal that spending is a medium of expression with consequences for long-term security.

The emotional undertone of this self-expressive spending cannot be overlooked. When purchases are questioned or judged, people often feel personally attacked, as if their identity has been challenged. A criticism of one's car or home décor is rarely heard as a critique of financial decision-making alone; it is experienced as a critique of self. This explains why discussions about money can be so fraught, particularly in families or relationships. Spending is not just about economics; it is about who we believe ourselves to be.

From a psychological perspective, the role of self-expression in spending ties closely to theories of symbolic interactionism, which argue that people construct identity through interaction and symbols. Money provides some of the most powerful symbols available in modern society. What we choose to buy, display, or avoid becomes part of our symbolic vocabulary. The difficulty is that this vocabulary is shaped heavily by cultural industries that profit from steering identity through consumption. Advertising does not only sell products; it sells aspirational selves. Brands do not only offer goods; they offer identities ready to be adopted. In this way, the expressive function of spending is constantly manipulated by external forces, often without awareness.

Recognising spending as self-expression is not simply an intellectual exercise; it has practical implications for financial wellbeing. When people mistake consumption for authenticity, they risk tethering identity to financial instability. If belonging requires constant expenditure, the result is anxiety rather than comfort. If individuality requires endless novelty, the result is depletion rather than fulfilment. The challenge, then, is to distinguish between authentic self-expression through spending and externally imposed scripts that masquerade as self-expression. *The difference lies in intention and awareness.* Purchases aligned with deeply held values can enhance identity; purchases driven by insecurity or pressure often erode it.

Ultimately, spending is one of the most visible ways in which people write their personal stories into the world. Every object owned, every experience chosen, becomes part of a narrative about selfhood. The power of money in shaping these narratives is undeniable, but so is the risk of surrendering agency to cultural and emotional forces that exploit the need for expression. By bringing awareness to the expressive function of spending, individuals can reclaim authorship of their financial lives, ensuring that their money reflects not just the identities they are sold but the identities they truly seek to embody.

Debt as Emotional Armor

Debt is usually framed as a numerical problem: too many loans, too much interest, not enough income to keep pace with repayments. Yet beneath the arithmetic lies something more profound. For many people, debt functions less as a financial instrument and more as a psychological shield. It becomes a form of emotional armour, allowing individuals to mask insecurities, preserve appearances, and project an image of stability or success that feels safer than exposing vulnerability. The paradox is that this armour, intended to protect, often inflicts deeper wounds. It preserves dignity in the short term while compounding anxiety in the long term, creating a cycle where the very strategy of protection intensifies the problem it seeks to solve.

The social dimension of debt is a critical part of this story. In societies where success is measured by visible prosperity, debt allows people to "keep up" when earnings alone would not suffice. A credit card can finance the fashionable wardrobe, the luxury car, or the holiday abroad that signals belonging to a peer group or professional class. For some, debt is less about access to goods than access to status. It provides a temporary ticket into circles where appearance carries weight, from corporate environments to social networks mediated by carefully curated online images. To admit that one cannot afford these symbols risks exclusion or humiliation. Debt, therefore, is not only a financial tool but also a means of self-preservation in a culture that equates worth with wealth.

This protective role is particularly evident in contexts of insecurity. Someone who feels inadequate in their career may compensate by purchasing expensive technology or clothing to project competence. A parent who worries about not giving their children the same opportunities as peers may overextend themselves on private schooling or extracurricular activities. A young adult uncertain about their place in the world may take on debt to fund travel or experiences that signal independence and adventure. In each case, debt is used to construct an identity narrative that counterbalances insecurity. It is, in effect, a costume of confidence worn in a world that punishes exposure.

The irony is that debt rarely relieves the underlying insecurity. Instead, it often magnifies it. The professional projecting success through visible consumption may lie awake at night calculating minimum payments. The parent striving to appear generous may feel suffocated by silent worry. The young adult chasing experiences may feel haunted by the shadow of repayments. The armour works in public but corrodes in private. What makes this cycle so pernicious is its self-reinforcing character: the greater the anxiety caused by debt, the stronger the temptation to borrow further to maintain appearances. To show weakness by cutting back feels riskier than to quietly take on more debt. Thus, the armour thickens even as it grows heavier.

Debt as emotional armour is also shaped by cultural narratives about masculinity, femininity, and adulthood. Men, socialised to equate financial provision with strength, may resort to borrowing rather than admitting difficulty, seeing disclosure as emasculating. Women, who often face competing pressures to appear generous, nurturing, and stylish, may conceal debts accrued in the attempt to meet these expectations. Young adults are often told that milestones such as owning a home, driving a car, or hosting lavish celebrations are markers of maturity, leading them to borrow heavily to signal that they have "arrived." In each case, debt disguises vulnerability while silently reinforcing it. *The emotional script dictates that it is better to borrow than to appear deficient.*

Historical and anthropological perspectives reveal that this phenomenon is not new, though its forms vary. In Victorian Britain, families often went into debt to maintain appearances of respectability—keeping a household with servants, hosting dinners, or dressing appropriately for their class, even when income did not support it. In contemporary contexts, the dynamic is amplified by credit systems that make borrowing seamless and by social media that multiplies the pressure to perform prosperity. Where once a neighbour's opinion might have mattered, now global audiences amplify the stage on which identities are performed. The armour must shine more brightly than ever, even if it is rusting underneath.

The emotional armour metaphor also explains why debt is so resistant to purely rational interventions. Financial education alone rarely changes behaviour, because the issue is not ignorance but identity. A person who uses debt to preserve dignity or belonging is unlikely to change merely because they learn about compound interest. The numbers are secondary to the role debt plays in maintaining psychological equilibrium. Telling someone to "cut up their credit card" without addressing the emotional meaning of that card is like asking them to remove their shield in battle. Without an alternative form of protection, the demand feels unbearable.

This helps explain the phenomenon of denial and secrecy around debt. People who use debt as armour often conceal the extent of their borrowing, even from partners or close family. To reveal the truth would be to admit the fragility that debt is designed to hide. They may juggle multiple credit lines, refinance to delay reckoning, or pay just enough to maintain the façade of control. These behaviours are not signs of irrationality but of desperation to keep the armour intact. The secrecy protects identity in the short term, but it corrodes trust and compounds isolation.

There is also a philosophical dimension to this dynamic. Debt as armour reveals the tension between appearance and reality in human life. Humans crave authenticity, yet they also crave acceptance. Money allows for the performance of authenticity—a curated self that looks confident, generous, or successful. But when that performance is financed by debt, the gap between appearance and reality widens. The armour becomes less a symbol of strength than a prison, forcing individuals to maintain a façade that isolates them from true connection. It is a stark reminder that when identity depends on external symbols, the cost is rarely limited to pounds and pence.

Counter-examples exist, and they are instructive. Some individuals face financial difficulty by stripping away the armour rather than reinforcing it. They downsize visibly, admit their struggles openly, or reject the status competition that fuels borrowing. Paradoxically, this vulnerability often leads to greater resilience. By refusing to rely on debt for protection, they discover alternative sources of dignity—relationships, creativity, or values that do not depend on material display. Their lives suggest that the antidote to debt as emotional armour is not austerity alone but authenticity: aligning spending with genuine priorities rather than external expectations.

To understand debt as emotional armour is to recognise that its costs cannot be measured on a balance sheet alone. The interest paid is only part of the burden. The greater cost is psychological: the anxiety of concealment, the erosion of authenticity, and the isolation that comes from living behind a façade. Yet it also opens the possibility of transformation. By naming the armour for what it is, individuals gain the power to choose whether to keep carrying it. Awareness is the first crack in the shield, the beginning of shifting from borrowed appearances to lived authenticity. Debt ceases to be armour when people find other, healthier ways to protect their dignity and express their worth.

Chapter 4
The Culture of Consumption

Walk through any high street, scroll through any social feed, or glance at the advertisements that line public transport, and you are reminded of a truth so pervasive it is rarely questioned: consumption is not only about meeting needs; it is about signalling worth. The culture of consumption does not simply offer goods and services for purchase; it scripts identities, orchestrates desires, and measures belonging. It insists that to live well is to acquire, to display, and to keep pace with an ever-accelerating rhythm of novelty. The material artefacts of this culture—a new phone, a larger home, a sleeker car—are presented as milestones of success, not just possessions. In this landscape, the question is no longer whether one consumes but how one consumes, and what those choices communicate to others.

What distinguishes modern consumer culture from earlier systems of trade and exchange is the intensity of manufactured desire. Advertising does not merely inform; it manipulates, crafting associations between products and emotions as though the two were inseparable. A car is never only about transport; it becomes a story about freedom, masculinity, or sophistication. A bottle of perfume is not positioned as scented liquid but as allure and desirability captured in glass. Social media intensifies this machinery by collapsing the boundary between advertising and daily life. Influencers, often under the guise of authenticity, weave consumption into narratives of beauty, success, and belonging, turning personal moments into commercial theatre. The result is a world in which *want* feels indistinguishable from *need.*

The psychological mechanism driving this system is comparison. Humans have always looked to others for cues on how to live, but the scale and immediacy of modern comparison is unprecedented. Where once neighbours or colleagues provided the benchmark, now millions of curated lives flash across screens in real time. The comparisons are rarely neutral: they tilt towards aspiration, featuring luxury holidays, designer wardrobes, and meticulously staged homes. The effect is both numbing and insidious: ordinary lives, however comfortable, feel lacking. Studies consistently show that financial satisfaction is less correlated with absolute income than with relative standing. A person may earn a stable, even generous salary, yet feel inadequate if surrounded by peers who appear to earn and display more. *Comparison becomes a currency of its own, and one perpetually in deficit.*

The cultural pressure to perform wealth exacerbates this trap. Beyond comparison lies expectation—the scripts that dictate what success should look like. In many societies, adulthood is narrated through financial milestones: the first home, the wedding, the car upgrade, the international holiday. Each comes with its own industry eager to supply goods and services that are marketed as necessities rather than choices. The dream home is not only shelter but a measure of ambition. The luxury car is not only transportation but a token of achievement. Designer goods are not only possessions but proof of refinement. These expectations are seductive precisely because they cloak themselves in normalcy: to decline them can feel like rejecting not just an object but a life stage. Yet the cost of compliance is often debt, overwork, or financial fragility.

The consequences ripple beyond individual households. When cultural scripts normalise perpetual consumption, societies orient around growth at any cost, tying wellbeing to economic expansion rather than genuine fulfilment. This orientation distorts priorities: healthcare, education, and community investments are often neglected in favour of consumer-driven policies that encourage spending above saving. At the personal level, individuals may sacrifice security for spectacle, deferring long-term stability to satisfy the immediate demand for display. In such an environment, financial distress is not a mark of personal irresponsibility alone but a predictable outcome of systemic pressure.

And yet, the possibility of liberation exists in the act of recognition. To see consumption as culturally scripted rather than purely personal is to regain a measure of agency. Once the manufactured nature of desire is understood, the compulsion to comply weakens. People who recognise that advertising equates consumption with worth can question whether the worth is real or imposed. Those who see comparison as a trap can begin to measure success by internal values rather than external signals. Families who interrogate the necessity of cultural milestones may choose alternatives that align with their financial reality rather than default expectations. *Breaking the script of "more" is less about renunciation than about reframing: wealth as sufficiency, status as self-defined, progress as freedom rather than accumulation.*

This chapter examines how the culture of consumption shapes not only spending but identity, belonging, and self-worth. It interrogates the machinery that manufactures desire, the comparisons that keep satisfaction perpetually out of reach, and the narratives that trap people in financial performance. At its heart lies a provocation: if consumption is culture's chosen script, then the most radical act is to question the script itself. To do so is not to reject material life but to reclaim it, to shift from being authored by culture to becoming the author of one's financial and emotional world.

The Manufactured Desire Machine

The modern economy does not simply provide goods; it engineers longings. Consumption is no longer tethered primarily to need or utility but to carefully cultivated feelings of insufficiency. Advertising, social media, and influencer culture collaborate in a vast apparatus designed to blur the line between want and necessity, conditioning individuals to equate spending with self-worth. This system is so pervasive that it often becomes invisible, woven into the fabric of daily life until people no longer ask whether they *need* something, but whether not having it implies they are inadequate. The manufactured desire machine does not merely sell products—it sells identities, aspirations, and validation.

Advertising has always sought to persuade, but in its earliest forms it largely emphasised function. Soap was cleaner, a tool sturdier, food fresher. Over the last century, however, the focus shifted decisively away from utility to symbolism. A car was no longer only about transport; it became a representation of freedom, virility, or sophistication. A pair of shoes ceased to be a means of protection for the feet; it became an emblem of style, belonging, and desirability. This shift was not incidental—it was strategic. By linking consumption to emotions and identity, marketers created an endless reservoir of demand. Once products could be positioned as proxies for self-esteem, status, or love, the appetite for them became insatiable. *It is not possible to "have enough" of identity, pride, or validation.*

In the age of social media, this machinery has been placed on steroids. Platforms built for connection became theatres of performance, where curated displays of lifestyle doubled as advertising. The influencer emerged as a hybrid figure: part peer, part brand ambassador, cloaking commercial persuasion in the guise of authenticity. A holiday photo, a morning skincare routine, a coffee order—each could be monetised as content, subtly nudging audiences to replicate not just the act but the purchase behind it. The genius of this model lies in its blurring of boundaries: persuasion becomes indistinguishable from everyday life. The message is clear yet unspoken: to be likeable, desirable, and worthy, one must consume in particular ways.

The impact of such conditioning is not confined to luxury goods. It infiltrates mundane decisions, shaping what we eat, wear, watch, and aspire to. Consider the way food delivery apps, framed through cheerful convenience, normalise constant spending on meals that previous generations would have reserved for rare occasions. Or the way smartphone upgrades, marketed through a mix of aspirational imagery and fear of obsolescence, make perfectly functional devices feel inadequate. These are not trivial indulgences; they are evidence of a system that teaches individuals to align their sense of progress with the frequency of their purchases. The product is almost secondary; what matters is the cycle of desire, satisfaction, and renewed longing that ensures the consumer never rests.

The psychological mechanisms underpinning this cycle are well understood by those who profit from it. One is the exploitation of social proof: humans are acutely attuned to what others are doing, and seeing peers consume a product powerfully signals that it is desirable or necessary. Another is the deliberate triggering of scarcity and urgency—limited-time offers, exclusive drops, countdown clocks—that hijack the brain's fear of missing out. Perhaps the most insidious is the alignment of brands with moral or social identity: to buy ethically sourced coffee or sustainable trainers is not just to purchase an item but to assert one's virtue. In this way, the manufactured desire machine colonises not just aesthetic aspiration but moral identity, making consumption feel like participation in a greater cause.

Real-world consequences flow from this conditioning. Financial stress rises when people attempt to keep pace with cultural expectations of consumption, yet the stress is often misattributed. A young professional, for example, may blame themselves for "poor budgeting" when in fact their choices are shaped by relentless exposure to messages that equate success with visible spending. Families may stretch mortgages to buy larger homes not solely because of space requirements but because cultural scripts have equated property size with achievement. Teenagers may feel anxious or excluded if they lack particular trainers or technology, mistaking absence of brand alignment for absence of identity. *The shame of not consuming "correctly" is as powerful as the pride of consuming well.*

And yet, it is important to recognise that this machinery works not simply because it is imposed from outside but because it aligns with deep human vulnerabilities. The desire to belong, to be admired, to feel secure, to reduce uncertainty—these are universal drives. Advertising and influencer culture succeed because they have learned to attach themselves to these needs with precision. The result is not that people are duped into wanting things they do not care about, but that their genuine needs for identity, love, or validation are rerouted through consumption. This explains why rational appeals to "spend less" or "ignore the adverts" are largely ineffective: they fail to address the underlying emotional resonance that makes the system compelling.

There are, however, cracks in the machine. Awareness is itself a form of resistance. Individuals who learn to see advertising as a carefully crafted manipulation can begin to decouple identity from consumption. Social movements that critique overconsumption or highlight its environmental consequences can erode the glamour once attached to endless acquisition. Younger generations, in particular, display ambivalence towards traditional markers of consumption, often valuing experiences or sustainability over sheer accumulation. But even these shifts are precarious, as industries quickly repackage anti-consumption values into new forms of consumable identity. Minimalism, for example, became its own profitable aesthetic, complete with purchasable accessories. The machine adapts.

The task, then, is not merely to condemn advertising or social media but to understand their mechanisms with clarity. By doing so, individuals and societies can create counter-narratives that privilege sufficiency over excess, meaning over display, and agency over manipulation. This does not mean rejecting consumption altogether—goods and services are necessary, and many enhance life immeasurably. But it does mean refusing to allow worth to be dictated by what one buys, wears, or posts. The manufactured desire machine is powerful precisely because it operates unseen; once illuminated, its influence becomes less absolute. *To question the script is to take the first step towards writing one's own.*

Comparison as Currency

Few forces in human psychology are as quietly corrosive as comparison. Money, which might otherwise function as a tool for exchange and security, is often transformed into a social scoreboard, measuring not only what one can afford but also how one appears in relation to others. This dynamic explains why two people on identical incomes may experience vastly different levels of satisfaction, depending less on what they actually possess and more on how their circumstances rank against those around them. Financial success becomes relative, not absolute. The trap lies in the endlessness of this metric: there will always be someone wealthier, more visibly successful, or apparently freer, ensuring that comparison functions as a perpetual source of dissatisfaction.

Psychologists have long recognised this as a variant of what is called the "relative income hypothesis." Studies demonstrate that people do not simply evaluate their earnings in isolation but assess them against the earnings of peers, neighbours, or colleagues. A seminal piece of research by economist Richard Easterlin highlighted that increases in national income do not necessarily translate into higher average happiness once basic needs are met, because expectations and comparisons rise in parallel. This is not merely a statistical quirk—it is a lived reality. Consider two professionals: one earning £60,000 in a community where most neighbours earn £40,000, and another earning £80,000 where the prevailing average is £120,000. Despite the objective difference, the first individual often reports higher satisfaction. The logic of comparison reshapes perception, such that status eclipses sufficiency. *People are less concerned with what they have than with whether they feel they have enough in relation to others.*

Social media has accelerated and intensified this phenomenon in ways earlier generations could scarcely imagine. Where once comparison might have been limited to local acquaintances or extended family, now it is global, instantaneous, and curated for impact. Platforms normalise constant exposure to others' highlight reels: holidays in exotic locations, luxury purchases, professional achievements, or seemingly effortless lifestyles. Crucially, these displays are not neutral—they are engineered for maximum impression, often hiding the debts, insecurities, or compromises beneath. Yet the psychological effect remains potent. Observing others' curated prosperity triggers a reflexive evaluation of one's own position, often leading to feelings of inadequacy even among those objectively well-off. The old adage that "keeping up with the Joneses" once referred to one's literal neighbours; today the "Joneses" are a billion strangers online.

Real-world examples illustrate the costs of this dynamic. A young lawyer earning a six-figure salary may nonetheless feel behind because peers are posting photos of homeownership, weddings, or international travel, prompting unnecessary spending to "catch up." A family comfortable on a middle income might overextend themselves with a larger house or car to match the perceived standard of their peer group, despite the strain this places on long-term stability. In each case, the issue is not material insufficiency but perceived social inferiority. Comparison transforms discretionary spending into obligatory outlay, eroding financial wellbeing in pursuit of a fleeting sense of parity.

The cultural glorification of success compounds this effect by equating visible wealth with personal worth. When society valorises those who display symbols of affluence—luxury brands, prestigious schools, exclusive memberships—it sets the benchmark for what is considered "enough." This is not simply a matter of aspiration but of pressure. Individuals feel judged not only by what they achieve but by what they can show. The consequence is a distortion of priorities: investments in appearance and lifestyle often supersede investments in security or fulfilment. A professional might delay saving for retirement to maintain a façade of present-day success; a parent might stretch finances to provide children with experiences deemed socially acceptable. In each instance, money is stripped of its instrumental role and redeployed as currency in the economy of comparison.

Philosophically, the problem lies in the way comparison externalises the measure of value. Instead of asking, "Does this serve my needs or reflect my values?" the underlying question becomes, "How does this make me look relative to others?" This shift erodes autonomy, because one's financial decisions are no longer anchored in internal priorities but dictated by the shifting and uncontrollable standards of a social group. *Comparison substitutes external validation for internal clarity, trapping individuals in cycles of expenditure that may not align with their actual desires.* The paradox is that, while comparison is often driven by the pursuit of esteem, it typically produces the opposite—restlessness, envy, and self-doubt.

There are, of course, counterpoints worth noting. Some argue that comparison can function as motivation, inspiring individuals to strive for greater success or higher standards. Seeing others achieve might encourage ambition, innovation, or perseverance. But the evidence suggests that such benefits are context-dependent and often short-lived. Where comparisons highlight achievable goals within one's control, they can indeed energise. Yet where comparisons involve unattainable lifestyles or obscure the sacrifices behind them, they breed frustration rather than fulfilment. The critical distinction is whether comparison informs genuine growth or coerces conformity to standards that may be ill-suited to one's circumstances.

Modern workplaces exemplify this tension vividly. Salary transparency, for example, is intended to promote fairness, yet it can also amplify dissatisfaction. Employees may feel undervalued when they discover peers earn more, even if their own salary remains adequate. Similarly, industries with visible markers of success—bonuses, promotions, awards—often cultivate cultures where value is conflated with outpacing others. While such systems can drive performance, they can also encourage unhealthy competition, burnout, and distorted definitions of achievement. Once again, comparison transforms money from a tool into a metric of identity, binding self-worth to relative standing rather than personal sufficiency.

Breaking free from comparison requires both awareness and intentionality. Awareness involves recognising the mechanics of social influence—the way platforms, advertising, and cultural scripts amplify comparison pressures. Intentionality involves redefining success on one's own terms, resisting the automatic equation of visibility with value. Some practical expressions of this include cultivating gratitude for sufficiency, anchoring financial decisions in long-term priorities rather than short-term impressions, and consciously limiting exposure to environments that fuel unnecessary competition. These are not easy shifts, given the ubiquity of the manufactured desire machine, but they are essential if money is to serve as a tool of autonomy rather than a trap of perpetual ranking.

Ultimately, the tragedy of comparison is its capacity to make abundance feel like lack. It transforms comfort into insufficiency, opportunity into disappointment, security into restlessness. It ensures that no matter how far one climbs, there is always another rung to measure against, another neighbour or colleague whose life seems brighter. By treating financial success as relative currency, individuals surrender control over satisfaction to forces beyond their reach. To reclaim that control requires disentangling worth from wealth's display, recognising that the only measure that truly matters is whether money is serving life—not whether it is outperforming someone else's.

The Pressure to Perform Wealth

One of the most powerful forces shaping financial behaviour today is not necessity but performance. The expectation is no longer merely to have enough, but to *show* that one has enough, and ideally more than enough. The cultural scripts of affluence—homeownership in a certain postcode, the gleaming car in the driveway, wardrobes populated with designer labels—have evolved from aspirational milestones into social obligations. Yet beneath the surface of these symbols lies a paradox: the very markers meant to signify prosperity often entrench financial fragility. The performance of wealth, rather than its careful cultivation, becomes the focal point, leaving individuals locked in cycles of debt, insecurity, and dissatisfaction.

The roots of this phenomenon stretch deep into collective psychology. Societies have long tied status to visible markers of success, from landownership in feudal Europe to elaborate dowries in traditional cultures. Today, however, the intensity and ubiquity of such expectations are magnified by consumer capitalism and digital display. Advertising primes individuals from childhood to associate luxury goods with belonging, respect, and desirability. Social media reinforces these cues by transforming life into a stage where curated lifestyles are not just shown but judged. The consequence is that financial decisions, which might otherwise be guided by prudence or personal value, are frequently subordinated to the imperative of display. *To be seen as prosperous often outweighs the actual experience of being financially secure.*

Consider the "dream home." In theory, it represents stability, security, and personal success. In practice, for many families it becomes a financial anchor that strains budgets and prolongs indebtedness. The cultural insistence that adulthood or achievement is incomplete without property ownership drives individuals to purchase beyond their means, stretching mortgages to the maximum allowable limit. What begins as a milestone of pride quickly morphs into a source of chronic stress, as earnings are consumed not by flexibility or opportunity but by the weight of servicing an oversized loan. Similarly, the purchase of luxury cars—often financed through complex leasing agreements—functions less as a transportation decision than as a performance of status. The vehicle becomes a rolling declaration of identity, but one that depreciates rapidly while extracting ongoing financial commitments.

This is not limited to high-net-worth symbols. Even relatively modest items, when linked to narratives of identity, exert a disproportionate hold over decision-making. Designer trainers for teenagers, high-end technology upgrades every year, weddings whose costs rival annual salaries—all operate as rituals of financial performance. Each purchase is rationalised not only by its utility but by its symbolic power: to fit in, to demonstrate love, to signal success. The deeper issue is not the purchase itself but the underlying compulsion: when spending is governed by external narratives rather than internal priorities, individuals cede control over their financial wellbeing.

The academic literature on conspicuous consumption, pioneered by Thorstein Veblen in the late nineteenth century, provides a framework for understanding these dynamics. Veblen observed that individuals consume not simply for use but for display, signalling their social position through visible expenditure. His insights remain strikingly relevant today, but modern variations add new complexity. Where Veblen described the leisure class flaunting wealth to distinguish themselves, today the pressure is democratised. Even those far from elite status feel compelled to perform prosperity. Credit markets have facilitated this shift by making debt widely available, enabling the performance of wealth without the foundation of wealth. *The appearance of prosperity becomes decoupled from its reality, yet the costs remain painfully tangible.*

The psychological consequences of this performance culture are profound. Individuals experience dissonance when their outward display of success masks inner instability. Financial stress coexists with social approval, creating a dangerous silence. A family admired for its spacious home may be quietly suffocating under mortgage repayments; a professional envied for designer suits may be living on a fragile line of credit. This incongruence fosters shame, secrecy, and denial, making it harder to seek help or recalibrate. In this sense, the performance of wealth not only drains financial resources but also erodes psychological resilience.

There is also a generational dimension. Young adults, especially in urban centres, often feel immense pressure to replicate the lifestyle markers of their parents or peers, despite radically different economic realities. Housing markets, student debt, and stagnant wages collide with cultural scripts that still promote homeownership, car ownership, and lavish consumption as benchmarks of maturity. The mismatch generates both frustration and peril: frustration at the difficulty of meeting these expectations, and peril when individuals attempt to bridge the gap through debt or unsustainable commitments. The result is a generation that may appear affluent on the surface but is more financially precarious than the one before it.

Counterarguments sometimes suggest that visible consumption can inspire ambition, motivating individuals to strive for success. Yet this perspective ignores the structural trap: striving may indeed lead some to genuine prosperity, but for many it results in cycles of overextension and disappointment. More importantly, the cultural script itself defines success narrowly, equating it with ownership and display rather than with security, autonomy, or wellbeing. This skewed definition ensures that even those who achieve the prescribed markers often find them hollow, discovering that the mortgage, the car, or the goods do not deliver the fulfilment promised.

Breaking free from the pressure to perform wealth requires interrogating these scripts at their core. Why is the dream home considered a universal goal, rather than one option among many? Why is the luxury car elevated as a marker of achievement, rather than financial independence or the freedom to pursue meaningful work? Why should a wedding's expense be read as a measure of love? These are not idle questions but essential ones, because cultural narratives, unless challenged, become internalised as personal truths. *To live without questioning them is to live in service to a script one never consciously chose.*

Practical resistance begins with redefining value. Instead of asking, "What will others think of this purchase?" one might ask, "What does this contribute to my life?" Such a shift reclaims agency by anchoring financial decisions in personal priorities rather than collective expectation. It also involves cultivating resilience against the psychological pull of status symbols—recognising, for instance, that admiration for visible consumption often fades quickly, while the financial strain lingers. Some individuals find success in deliberately opting out of certain scripts, choosing smaller homes, modest cars, or unconventional career paths, not as sacrifices but as affirmations of autonomy. Their lives may look less impressive on Instagram, but they are often richer in freedom and security.

The larger cultural shift requires broader conversations about the narratives we endorse. Media, education, and policy all play roles in either perpetuating or challenging the pressure to perform wealth. Financial literacy must extend beyond budgets and interest rates to include critical thinking about cultural scripts. The challenge is not only to teach people how to manage money but also how to interpret the forces that tell them what money should signify. Without this awareness, individuals remain vulnerable to traps that can ensnare even the highly educated and financially literate.

The irony of the pressure to perform wealth is that it undermines the very prosperity it seeks to convey. By prioritising appearance over substance, display over resilience, it ensures that many who look successful are in fact one setback away from collapse. Recognising and resisting these narratives does not mean rejecting aspiration or comfort; it means distinguishing between genuine fulfilment and the hollow pursuit of symbols. The ultimate measure of financial health is not how convincingly one can perform wealth, but how securely one can live free from its compulsions.

Breaking the Script of "More"

The most persistent illusion in modern economies is that happiness and fulfilment can be purchased through the accumulation of more—more income, more possessions, more experiences packaged for consumption. Yet the more people pursue "more," the less satisfied they tend to feel. This paradox is not incidental but structural: the cultural scripts that equate consumption with worth are designed to keep individuals striving indefinitely. Recognising and questioning these scripts is therefore not simply an exercise in financial literacy but a profound act of reclaiming autonomy. *Freedom begins not with another purchase but with the refusal to let purchasing define freedom itself.*

The script of "more" is deeply entrenched because it is subtle. Unlike explicit rules or laws, cultural scripts are absorbed through repetition, imitation, and social reinforcement. Children rarely need to be told that material accumulation signifies success; they observe it in the way adults praise certain possessions, in the attention given to wealthier neighbours, in the subtle envy that circulates around objects of status. By adulthood, the script has become second nature, shaping not only desires but also the metrics by which individuals measure themselves. A person may believe they are exercising free choice when upgrading a phone or renovating a kitchen, yet beneath the surface lies the unexamined pressure of a narrative that insists standing still is equivalent to falling behind.

The psychological consequences of this narrative are well documented. Behavioural economics highlights the concept of the "hedonic treadmill": individuals rapidly adapt to higher levels of consumption, such that what once felt like abundance soon becomes the new baseline. The excitement of acquisition fades, leaving only the need for further acquisition. The treadmill effect ensures that "more" never feels sufficient, fuelling dissatisfaction even among those with substantial resources. This helps explain why financial stress is not limited to those on low incomes. A professional earning six figures may feel just as anxious about money as someone earning far less, because the script of "more" constantly raises the standard of what counts as enough. *The scarcity is not material but psychological, born from comparison and expectation rather than need.*

Real-world examples illustrate how destructive this cycle can be. Consider the phenomenon of lifestyle inflation: as income increases, spending often rises in tandem, cancelling out the potential for greater security. An individual might move from renting a modest flat to purchasing a larger home, only to discover that the mortgage, maintenance, and social expectations tether them more tightly to financial anxiety. Holidays, cars, and leisure activities scale upward, each framed as the rightful reward for hard work, yet together they erode the very stability they were meant to symbolise. The cultural script whispers that restraint is failure, that settling for "less" signals inadequacy. Thus, the pursuit of more becomes not merely a financial pattern but an identity imperative.

The irony is that questioning the script of "more" often leads to greater satisfaction. Research in psychology consistently shows that beyond a certain threshold—enough to cover basic needs and a modest margin for security—additional consumption contributes little to wellbeing. Experiences, relationships, and autonomy matter far more than material accumulation. Yet cultural narratives invert this truth, elevating possessions as the visible evidence of a successful life. To resist these narratives requires both courage and clarity: courage to deviate from the expectations of peers and family, and clarity to redefine success in terms that are personally meaningful rather than culturally imposed.

Take, for example, the movement towards minimalism or voluntary simplicity. Although sometimes caricatured as aesthetic choices, these practices are better understood as conscious rejections of the script of "more." Individuals who adopt them often describe a sense of relief, discovering that owning fewer possessions liberates time, energy, and financial resources. They are not necessarily rejecting comfort or aspiration, but they are refusing the idea that value must be proven through accumulation. Their decisions reflect a deliberate reframing: success is measured not by the size of the house but by the absence of financial anxiety; not by the newest gadget but by the capacity to choose how time is spent.

Breaking the script does not mean abandoning ambition. Rather, it means interrogating ambition to ensure it serves the individual rather than the culture of consumption. One can pursue professional growth, creativity, or even financial prosperity without succumbing to the imperative of constant display. The difference lies in motivation: is the pursuit grounded in authentic goals or in the desire to meet external benchmarks? A lawyer who chooses to work fewer hours to spend time with family, even at the cost of a smaller home, is no less ambitious than one who climbs the corporate ladder to finance luxury. The former may, in fact, be exercising a deeper form of ambition—the ambition to live a life aligned with values rather than appearances.

The obstacles to such reframing are formidable. Advertising industries invest billions in ensuring that individuals feel inadequate without the next purchase. Social media algorithms amplify images of luxury and success, curating feeds that equate self-worth with consumption. Peer pressure, too, remains potent; to say no to cultural scripts is to risk exclusion, to invite the judgement of those still bound to them. Yet history shows that cultural scripts are not immutable. Practices once considered essential—such as dowries, rigid dress codes, or ostentatious public feasts—have faded with time as societies redefined value. The script of "more" can likewise be rewritten, but it requires both individual resistance and collective conversation.

Philosophical traditions across cultures provide insight here. Stoic thinkers in ancient Greece emphasised the importance of distinguishing between what is within one's control and what is not, urging detachment from the endless pursuit of external goods. Buddhist teachings similarly caution against craving, framing it as a source of suffering. Even modern secular ethics highlight the virtues of moderation and sustainability. These traditions converge on a simple truth: *freedom lies not in accumulation but in the mastery of desire.* Recognising this truth in a consumer-driven age is radical, yet it is also liberating.

The practical implications of breaking the script are profound. Individuals who consciously step back from the compulsion to pursue more often find themselves better positioned to build financial resilience. Savings accumulate not because of deprivation but because spending is guided by intention rather than impulse. Debt diminishes, not through rigid austerity, but through the refusal to purchase symbols of status that do not align with genuine priorities. The psychological benefits are equally significant: reduced anxiety, greater satisfaction with what one already has, and a sense of empowerment that comes from living by choice rather than by script.

Perhaps the most striking aspect of rejecting "more" is that it opens space for alternative forms of wealth. Time becomes wealth when it is no longer surrendered to servicing debt or financing unnecessary consumption. Relationships deepen when they are not mediated by status competition. Creativity flourishes when resources are not drained by the constant chase for the latest product. These are forms of wealth that cannot be easily displayed on social media or measured by conventional metrics, yet they constitute the foundation of a genuinely prosperous life.

The cultural script of "more" thrives on silence; it remains powerful precisely because it is rarely questioned. To break it, individuals must articulate different stories about what matters—stories that prioritise autonomy, security, and meaning over accumulation. The shift begins privately, in the quiet recalibration of priorities, but it gains force collectively, as communities embrace alternative narratives. When enough people refuse to equate consumption with worth, the culture itself begins to shift.

The challenge, then, is not to escape culture altogether but to participate in reshaping it. By questioning the inevitability of "more," individuals reclaim the power to define enough for themselves. They step off the treadmill of comparison and enter a space where financial decisions reflect values rather than pressures. The act of breaking the script is therefore not only financial wisdom but cultural resistance. It dismantles the illusion that self-worth can be purchased and replaces it with the recognition that true prosperity is lived, not displayed.

Chapter 5
Self-Sabotage and Financial Loops

There is a peculiar irony at the heart of human behaviour: people can know exactly what undermines them financially, yet continue doing it. The individual who vows never again to rely on credit cards finds themselves swiping one at the first sign of stress. The person who swears they will begin saving seriously after their next pay rise discovers, yet again, that the increased income has already evaporated into lifestyle upgrades. These cycles rarely arise from ignorance. More often, they reflect the pull of unconscious habits and emotional safety—the comfort of familiar pain—where repetition feels less threatening than change, even if that repetition is destructive. *The difficulty is not in knowing better but in doing differently.*

Understanding these loops requires acknowledging how easily the human mind privileges familiarity over progress. Behavioural science demonstrates that predictability, even in negative forms, offers a strange sense of security. Someone accustomed to financial scarcity may repeatedly create conditions of shortfall, not out of preference but out of unconscious attachment to a state that feels known. It is a pattern observable in relationships, careers, and health, but nowhere is it more apparent than with money. The result is a life lived in cycles: paycheque to paycheque despite high income, debt repayments made only to be re-incurred, resolutions crafted and broken with uncanny similarity year after year. These repetitions are not coincidences but deeply coded responses shaped by psychology, stress, and cultural reinforcement.

Cognitive dissonance lies at the centre of these contradictions. People routinely profess that they value financial security, autonomy, or the ability to provide for family, yet enact behaviours that directly undermine those goals. The mental discomfort of this inconsistency is resolved not by changing behaviour but by adjusting rationalisations: *"I deserve this purchase after such a long week,"* or *"Life is short, so why not enjoy it now?"* In the moment, these justifications relieve tension, but they also ensure that dissonance remains unresolved, perpetuating the very habits that conflict with stated values. Over time, the gap between declared intention and enacted reality widens, and the identity of being "bad with money" begins to take root.

Stress intensifies these loops, narrowing decision-making capacity and tilting behaviour towards short-term relief rather than long-term planning. Neuroscience shows that financial anxiety activates the same neural pathways as physical threats, reducing cognitive bandwidth for complex reasoning. Under such strain, the human brain prioritises immediate comfort—purchases that soothe, avoidance of bills that feel overwhelming, distractions that delay accountability. Each choice might bring temporary relief, but it deepens the underlying problem, creating a cycle where stress generates poor decisions, which in turn generate more stress. The individual, caught in this loop, often interprets the repetition as evidence of personal inadequacy, failing to see the structural and psychological forces at play.

When repeated often enough, these patterns crystallise into identity. A person who has cycled through overdrafts, impulsive spending, and financial regret may begin to narrate their life through the lens of inevitability: *"I'm simply irresponsible with money,"* or *"I'll never be the kind of person who can save."* These statements do more than describe; they prescribe. They shape behaviour by limiting the imagination of alternatives, making change feel not just difficult but incompatible with selfhood. In this way, loops become self-fulfilling. The more someone rehearses the identity of financial incompetence, the more they inhabit it, and the harder it becomes to see any possibility of transformation.

Breaking free demands more than practical advice about budgeting or investing. It requires exposing the underlying scripts, challenging the assumptions that familiarity equals safety, and reconstituting identity around the possibility of change rather than the certainty of repetition. To do so is to treat financial patterns not as immutable traits but as learned behaviours that can be unlearned. This chapter will interrogate the comfort of familiar pain, the pull of cognitive dissonance, the corrosive influence of stress, and the subtle process by which loops harden into identities. In doing so, it will illuminate why people so often work against their own financial interests—and how they can begin to rewrite those patterns into narratives of autonomy rather than sabotage.

The challenge is not merely to accumulate knowledge but to dismantle the emotional architecture that sustains destructive cycles. Once recognised, these loops lose some of their grip; what once seemed like inevitability can be reframed as choice. By the end of this exploration, the reader will see that financial self-sabotage is not evidence of weakness but of deeply human tendencies—tendencies that, once brought to light, can be redirected towards resilience, clarity, and freedom.

The Comfort of Familiar Pain

Few paradoxes are as striking as the persistence of financial mistakes among people who fully recognise their destructive consequences. The professional who repeatedly drains their savings with impulsive purchases, the household that cycles in and out of credit card debt despite solemn vows to stop, the individual who avoids opening bills until penalties accumulate—all of them illustrate the same truth: knowledge alone rarely interrupts entrenched behaviour. What compels a person to keep returning to circumstances that cause them stress, shame, and loss? The answer lies not in logic but in psychology: familiarity often feels safer than change, even when familiarity is painful. *The mind clings to what it knows, even when what it knows corrodes security and wellbeing.*

To understand this phenomenon, one must look beyond surface explanations of poor discipline or lack of willpower. Behavioural research consistently shows that repeated patterns are less about rational choice and more about deep emotional attachments to predictability. The brain has evolved to privilege certainty over risk; what is known—even if damaging—registers as less threatening than the unknown. For individuals raised in households marked by scarcity, debt, or financial volatility, repeated exposure to stress creates a baseline of normality. As adults, they may unconsciously replicate these conditions, not out of preference but because stability feels alien. The irony is that dysfunction, once rehearsed often enough, becomes its own form of security.

Consider the common case of someone who lives paycheque to paycheque despite earning a high income. When questioned, they may admit frustration at the cycle, yet find themselves unable to accumulate savings. Beneath the surface lies not ignorance about the benefits of saving but an ingrained comfort with immediate consumption. For years, money arriving and money disappearing quickly may have been the rhythm of life; the quiet accumulation of funds in an account feels disorienting, even unsafe. In psychological terms, the absence of familiar stress can itself generate anxiety, compelling people to recreate the very pressures they claim to despise. *Pain becomes comfortable not because it is desirable but because it is known.*

The persistence of familiar pain also reflects a basic truth about human identity: patterns become self-definitions. When people say, "I've always been bad with money" or "I'm just the kind of person who can't save," they are not merely describing behaviour; they are narrating a self-concept. That identity, once rehearsed, becomes a lens through which decisions are filtered. If I am "bad with money," then avoiding bills, overspending, or neglecting to save are not anomalies but confirmations of who I am. Breaking free of such an identity requires confronting not just habits but the deep comfort of a narrative that, while painful, is consistent and predictable. In this way, repetition protects identity even at the expense of wellbeing.

Stress compounds these dynamics. Neuroscientific research shows that stress narrows cognitive function, reducing the brain's ability to evaluate long-term consequences and biasing it toward immediate relief. For someone already caught in a cycle of financial struggle, the acute stress of unpaid bills or looming deadlines magnifies the impulse to escape through avoidance or indulgence. The purchase of a luxury item, the decision to ignore a financial statement, or the temporary high of an expensive night out may relieve stress in the moment, but they lock the individual into the same cycle that generated the stress in the first place. This looping mechanism makes change feel doubly threatening: not only does it require unfamiliar behaviour, it withholds the short-term relief to which the person has become accustomed.

The phenomenon is not confined to individuals of limited means. High earners are equally susceptible to the allure of familiar pain, albeit in more disguised forms. A surgeon may consistently overspend to match the lifestyle expectations of their peers, not because they fail to understand the mathematics of debt but because the risk of standing apart socially feels more threatening than financial strain. An entrepreneur may reinvest recklessly in ventures despite past failures because the thrill of high stakes is more familiar than the patience of long-term wealth building. In both cases, the comfort of operating within known psychological scripts outweighs the rational benefits of restraint.

Philosophically, the comfort of familiar pain underscores the tension between freedom and determinism in human behaviour. On one level, individuals appear free to choose differently: to save instead of spend, to plan instead of improvise, to face rather than avoid. Yet on another level, their choices are powerfully shaped by unconscious attachments to what they have always known. Change, even positive change, disrupts the continuity of self. To move from scarcity to stability is not just a financial shift but an existential one, requiring the person to inhabit an identity they have not rehearsed. It is not surprising, then, that people retreat to old loops: they are not merely choosing behaviours, they are defending a sense of self.

This insight has practical consequences. Financial advice that assumes rational actors—spreadsheets, budgets, logical persuasion—often fails because it does not address the underlying comfort with dysfunction. The more effective approach lies in helping individuals recognise the familiarity of their patterns, to see not only the cost of their choices but the psychological safety those choices provide. Once the comfort is named, it can be challenged. People can be guided to build new patterns of safety around behaviours that align with their stated goals: finding reassurance in a growing savings account, deriving pride from resisting social pressures, experiencing relief not in avoidance but in mastery. The key is not to strip away comfort but to re-anchor it in new behaviours.

Cultural narratives also reinforce the comfort of familiar pain. Entire industries—from credit providers to luxury branding—depend on people repeating financially harmful cycles. The language of "treat yourself" or "normal" debt creates a social permission structure that makes destructive repetition feel not only acceptable but expected. In such an environment, breaking away from familiar patterns requires countercultural courage. The person who resists lifestyle inflation, who embraces frugality, or who chooses security over display must also resist the discomfort of being seen as different. The pull back into familiar pain is not only internal but external, woven into cultural expectations that equate worth with visible spending.

The deeper challenge lies in reframing how people relate to change itself. Too often, change is perceived as loss: the loss of comfort, predictability, identity, or social belonging. By recognising this framing, individuals can begin to construct alternative narratives. Instead of seeing financial transformation as the abandonment of what is known, they can see it as the acquisition of a more expansive identity—one that includes resilience, control, and possibility. In this sense, breaking free from the comfort of familiar pain is less about rejecting the past than about integrating it into a broader story of growth.

Ultimately, the persistence of repeated mistakes is not evidence of irrationality so much as a testament to the power of the familiar. People will choose known discomfort over unknown freedom until they recognise that comfort is a poor substitute for wellbeing. Once seen clearly, the lure of repetition loses some of its hold. The challenge is to help individuals not only "know better" in the intellectual sense but to feel safe enough to act differently. Only then does the cycle of self-sabotage begin to loosen, replaced not by abstract ideals but by the tangible comfort of new, healthier patterns.

Cognitive Dissonance with Money

The human relationship with money is full of contradiction. Ask people what they want financially, and the answers often sound universal: security, independence, peace of mind. Yet observe their behaviour, and an entirely different picture emerges. Individuals who insist that stability is their goal might simultaneously indulge in spending sprees, neglect essential bills, or take on debt with little plan for repayment. This tension between stated intentions and actual actions is not merely hypocrisy or weakness; it is the product of *cognitive dissonance*, the psychological discomfort created when beliefs and behaviours collide. In the domain of money, this dissonance is both widespread and corrosive, shaping decisions in ways that erode the very outcomes people claim to desire.

Cognitive dissonance theory, first articulated by psychologist Leon Festinger in the 1950s, describes the mental strain that arises when a person holds conflicting beliefs or when actions contradict values. To relieve this strain, the individual either changes their behaviour, adjusts their beliefs, or rationalises the inconsistency. With money, rationalisation often wins. The person who believes in the virtue of financial prudence but spends extravagantly on a holiday may justify it by saying, "You only live once," or "I deserve this after working so hard." These narratives ease the tension in the moment but deepen the long-term conflict between aspiration and reality. *The mind seeks psychological comfort even at the expense of financial stability.*

What makes money particularly vulnerable to dissonance is its dual nature: it is both practical and symbolic. Practically, money represents the means to pay rent, buy food, and secure the future. Symbolically, it is tied to identity, status, desire, and belonging. The symbolic pull is often stronger than the practical logic, leading to choices that undermine security while affirming identity. For example, someone may say they value freedom from financial stress, yet they purchase a luxury car that locks them into years of debt repayments. The dissonance is resolved not by confronting the contradiction but by reinterpreting it—convincing themselves that the car is "an investment in image" or "necessary for confidence at work." Such reframing preserves self-concept while perpetuating financial vulnerability.

Case studies of this dynamic are everywhere. Consider the graduate who insists they want to be debt-free yet continues to fund a lifestyle on credit cards because "everyone my age does the same." Or the couple who declares that saving for a home is their priority, only to spend thousands on a lavish wedding justified as a "once-in-a-lifetime event." In each case, dissonance is managed by rationalisation rather than behaviour change. The relief is temporary;

the cycle continues. *What people say about money often reflects their ideals, while what they do reveals the emotional truths they are less willing to confront.*

The cultural environment magnifies these conflicts. Advertising and social media constantly feed messages that undermine stated financial goals. A person may genuinely believe that long-term security matters most, but the curated images of peers travelling, dining, or acquiring luxury goods trigger an immediate need to belong. Spending becomes a way to reconcile the discomfort of exclusion, even as it contradicts the deeper value of security. Here, cognitive dissonance is less an individual failing than a collective condition of modern consumer culture, where external pressures make inconsistency almost inevitable.

Psychological experiments further illustrate how dissonance operates in financial contexts. Studies on "mental accounting" show that people categorise money irrationally, treating a tax refund as "free money" even if they are in debt. The belief that one is financially responsible collides with the behaviour of spending recklessly in certain categories. The inconsistency is often resolved by compartmentalising: "I would never waste my salary, but bonuses are for fun." This preserves the self-image of responsibility while undermining the reality of financial health. The gap between belief and action remains intact, but the discomfort is hidden beneath mental gymnastics.

Stress and scarcity intensify dissonance. When under financial strain, individuals may claim that their highest priority is to escape debt, yet they reach for spending as a coping mechanism. The paradox is understandable: small indulgences provide psychological relief from stress, but they also deepen the very conditions that cause the stress. The mind resolves this contradiction by downplaying the cost: "It's just a coffee," "It's only a small treat," "This won't make a difference." Over time, the accumulation of such justifications perpetuates cycles that are both emotionally soothing and financially damaging.

An especially destructive form of cognitive dissonance emerges when people attach moral weight to money. Many believe they *should* save, budget, and plan, and when they fail, the dissonance creates not only discomfort but shame. Instead of addressing the mismatch directly, they avoid financial realities altogether—ignoring bank statements, delaying bill payments, or refusing to discuss money in relationships. Avoidance reduces the immediate discomfort of facing the inconsistency but ensures that the financial problem grows. The irony is that efforts to protect self-image from dissonance ultimately inflict greater harm on both finances and wellbeing.

There are, however, moments when cognitive dissonance can become a catalyst for positive change. The discomfort it generates is not inherently destructive; it is a signal that alignment is missing. Some individuals use that signal to re-examine their priorities, bringing behaviour into closer alignment with values. The person who repeatedly experiences regret after impulsive purchases may eventually use that regret to establish stricter boundaries, reframing the dissonance as evidence of growth. Likewise, couples who confront the gap between their stated goals and spending habits can use the tension to initiate difficult but transformative conversations. *The discomfort of dissonance can either entrench harmful loops or propel meaningful change, depending on how it is managed.*

Breaking free from destructive cycles of dissonance requires more than financial knowledge. Most people already know that overspending, neglecting bills, or accruing debt is unwise. What they need is the ability to recognise the dissonance in real time and resist the easy path of rationalisation. This might mean cultivating practices of reflection, such as pausing before purchases to ask whether the action matches stated goals, or discussing openly with trusted peers to expose rationalisations that thrive in secrecy. By deliberately bringing beliefs and actions into dialogue, individuals can begin to close the gap that dissonance creates.

Ultimately, cognitive dissonance with money is a mirror of the human condition. People long for security, yet they are also pulled by identity, belonging, and the pursuit of comfort. The tension between these forces is not a flaw but a feature of psychological life. The challenge lies in acknowledging the gap without surrendering to it—using the discomfort of inconsistency as a compass rather than a trap. The recognition that *what we say about money is not always what we do* is the first step toward bridging the distance between aspiration and reality. Once that bridge is built, financial decisions become less about managing contradictions and more about embodying coherence.

The Role of Stress in Bad Decisions

Few forces distort human judgment as effectively as stress, and nowhere is this more visible than in matters of money. Financial stress is not simply a feeling of unease; it is a cognitive burden that reduces attention, shortens time horizons, and narrows the field of perceived options. In moments of acute pressure—when bills pile up, when debt collectors call, or when an unexpected expense hits—people often make choices that directly undermine their longer-term goals. It is not that they do not know better; it is that the very capacity to think better is compromised. *Stress shrinks the mind's aperture, focusing attention on immediate relief at the expense of future stability.*

Research in behavioural economics and psychology has repeatedly demonstrated that scarcity—whether of money, time, or cognitive bandwidth—induces what scholars term a "tunnelling effect." Scarcity consumes mental resources, leaving less capacity for deliberate thought. Experiments by Sendhil Mullainathan and Eldar Shafir, for instance, reveal that individuals under financial strain perform worse on cognitive tests, not because they are less capable in general, but because part of their mental bandwidth is perpetually hijacked by worry. This impairment can be the difference between paying a bill on time or missing it, between considering a high-interest loan carefully or accepting it without reading the terms. In this sense, *stress does not merely coexist with poor financial decisions; it actively manufactures them.*

Real-world examples make this dynamic painfully clear. Consider payday lending: borrowers under stress often agree to exorbitant interest rates for the sake of immediate liquidity. The rational calculation—that borrowing £200 at 400% APR is financially ruinous—disappears under the cognitive weight of urgent need. The rent must be paid tomorrow, the fridge must be filled tonight; the cost next month is abstract, distant, and overshadowed by present panic. Similarly, individuals overwhelmed by debt often avoid opening letters from creditors or delay filing taxes. This is not laziness; it is a stress-induced coping mechanism. Avoidance feels like relief, if only for a moment, but ensures that the financial problem compounds.

The destructive cycle operates like this: stress narrows focus, leading to decisions that prioritise short-term relief. Those decisions create further negative consequences, which then amplify stress, further narrowing focus. Over time, the loop hardens into habit. The person begins to believe, "I'm bad with money," not recognising that their failures are less about character and more about the physiological effects of stress. Neuroscience shows that chronic stress elevates cortisol levels, impairing the prefrontal cortex—the region of the brain responsible for planning, impulse control, and rational judgment. The very biology of stress tilts decision-making towards the impulsive and away from the reflective.

It is tempting to view poor financial decisions under stress as failures of willpower, but such a view is misleading and unhelpful. What looks like irresponsibility from the outside is often a predictable response to the pressures of scarcity. For instance, someone with stable income may struggle to understand why a neighbour on a tight budget spends money on cigarettes or takeaway meals. Yet for the stressed individual, these small purchases provide immediate emotional relief. In the absence of hope for larger stability, momentary comfort becomes disproportionately valuable. *Stress does not just change what people choose; it changes what they perceive as worth choosing.*

The social context compounds the problem. Financial stress rarely occurs in isolation; it is often entangled with shame and secrecy. Many people under strain feel unable to admit their situation to friends, family, or employers, fearing judgement. This silence eliminates access to external perspectives that might break the stress loop. Instead, decisions are made in solitude, where cognitive distortions go unchallenged. Worse, stress-induced behaviours—such as borrowing more money to cover existing debts or ignoring financial correspondence—reinforce the conditions of scarcity that produced the stress in the first place. The loop is self-perpetuating not only at the psychological level but also at the structural level of obligations, interest rates, and penalties.

Yet there is another dimension worth noting: stress sometimes produces surprising clarity. In limited cases, acute pressure can sharpen focus on essentials, cutting through distractions. A household facing sudden redundancy might eliminate wasteful expenses overnight, finally aligning behaviour with stated goals. The paradox is that stress can both cloud judgment and catalyse decisive action, depending on how it is channelled. The distinction lies in whether stress narrows perception into tunnel vision or propels attention towards restructuring priorities. Most often, however, without deliberate intervention, the narrowing dominates, and destructive cycles continue.

Breaking the link between stress and bad financial decisions requires recognising that financial health is not just about literacy but also about psychology. Teaching people about compound interest, budgeting, or long-term investing is necessary but insufficient if stress is left unaddressed. Interventions that reduce cognitive load—automatic savings systems, debt consolidation, or even reminders designed to simplify choices—can create the mental space needed for better decisions. Likewise, practices such as mindfulness or reframing debt as a solvable challenge rather than an existential crisis can interrupt the stress-response loop. These are not luxuries; they are tools for restoring the mental bandwidth without which rational financial behaviour is almost impossible.

The philosophical lesson here is sobering. Human beings like to believe they are autonomous agents making deliberate choices, but financial stress exposes the fragility of that belief. When the nervous system is flooded with anxiety, freedom contracts. Choices become reactions, not reflections. Acknowledging this limitation is not disempowering; it is clarifying. It shows why cycles of financial distress are so difficult to escape and why judgmental attitudes toward those trapped in them are misplaced. *What appears to be irrationality is often the most rational response possible under the suffocating weight of stress.*

Understanding the role of stress in bad decisions shifts the conversation about money from one of moral failing to one of human limitation. It suggests that effective financial change must involve more than strategies and spreadsheets; it must also involve addressing the psychological load carried by those under pressure. Only then can people move from reactive decisions made in the heat of stress to deliberate choices aligned with their deeper values and longer-term aspirations. Recognising the destructive power of stress is the first step towards breaking the cycles it creates and reclaiming the capacity for financial clarity.

How Loops Become Identities

One of the most striking features of human behaviour is how repeated mistakes transform from isolated events into personal truths. In the realm of money, this process is particularly insidious. A missed bill, a rash purchase, or a cycle of borrowing can, through repetition, calcify into a story about the self: *I'm just bad with money.* What begins as a pattern of behaviour becomes a statement of identity, and once it is entrenched, it shapes future choices in ways that reinforce the very problem it describes.

The human mind is a meaning-making machine. It does not simply record events; it interprets them, weaving them into coherent narratives. These narratives give us stability and predictability, but they also restrict us. If a person consistently finds themselves overdrawn, paying late fees, or overspending despite resolutions not to, the brain naturally seeks to explain the pattern. The simplest explanation is internal: perhaps I lack discipline, perhaps I'm irresponsible, perhaps I'm just not built to handle money. Over time, this explanation hardens into identity, and identity is far harder to change than a single behaviour. *Once a loop becomes a label, the label begins to drive the loop.*

Psychologists have long noted the power of self-fulfilling prophecies. When someone believes they are inherently poor at mathematics, they avoid situations where their skills could improve, ensuring that the belief remains intact. Money functions in much the same way. The individual who says, "I'm hopeless with finances," may avoid budgeting apps, financial planning workshops, or even conversations with financially literate friends, because these situations threaten their identity. The avoidance means their skills never improve, and their financial difficulties continue, reinforcing the original belief. What began as a coping mechanism—explaining away failures—becomes a self-imposed barrier to growth.

Real-world examples illustrate how powerful this identity trap can be. Consider the professional earning a comfortable salary who nonetheless struggles with debt. Each month, they resolve to save more, yet each month the cycle repeats. Instead of seeing this as a solvable behavioural loop, they absorb it into their identity: *I'm a spender, not a saver.* Soon, they not only expect to overspend but even make choices consistent with that expectation. Buying the expensive dinner or ignoring the mounting credit card balance feels natural, because it aligns with the self-concept they have internalised. The identity becomes a script, directing actions without conscious deliberation.

Identity loops are further reinforced by culture and language. Friends jokingly describe someone as "terrible with money," family members repeat the same labels, and individuals begin to echo them in self-deprecating humour. These casual reinforcements cement the loop into a social identity as well as a private belief. The danger is that identity-based statements feel immutable. While one can change a habit, identities appear permanent. If overspending is framed as a flaw in behaviour, one can try new strategies; if overspending is framed as a flaw in character, change feels futile. *The difference between 'I overspent' and 'I'm a spender' is not semantic—it is psychological destiny.*

Philosophically, the issue raises questions about free will and self-determination. To what extent are we authors of our financial lives, and to what extent are we prisoners of the narratives we have inherited and constructed? It is not uncommon for someone to carry childhood messages—"we're not good with money in this family"—into adulthood, where they blend with personal failures to form an enduring identity. The irony is that these narratives feel like authentic self-knowledge, when in fact they are learned scripts reinforced by repetition. Recognising that identities are constructed rather than discovered is the first step toward rewriting them.

There is also a neurological basis for these loops. Habits, when repeated, carve neural pathways that make the behaviour easier to repeat next time. Over time, the habit requires less conscious energy to enact. Layer on top the psychological narrative—"this is who I am"—and the behaviour becomes doubly reinforced: biologically by habit, psychologically by identity. The combination is why financial self-sabotage often feels so intractable. People are not only fighting the momentum of behaviour but also the gravitational pull of self-concept.

The implications extend beyond personal finances to broader societal patterns. Studies show that individuals from low-income backgrounds are more likely to adopt self-limiting identities around money, not because they are inherently less capable, but because repeated exposure to scarcity, debt, and failure creates more opportunities for negative loops to become internalised. In such cases, identity traps perpetuate inequality. Someone who believes they are destined to be poor or financially incompetent is less likely to pursue opportunities, seek advice, or engage in long-term planning. Identity becomes not just a reflection of experience but a barrier to mobility.

There is, however, an important nuance: not all identity loops are destructive. Just as negative loops create limitations, positive ones can foster resilience. Someone who frames themselves as "disciplined with money" is more likely to act in ways that preserve that identity, resisting temptations and adhering to budgets. The lesson is not to abandon identity altogether but to recognise its power and ensure it is consciously chosen rather than unconsciously inherited. The challenge lies in shifting from a negative loop to a positive one—a process that requires both breaking old habits and reshaping self-concept.

Breaking identity loops is possible but demands more than behavioural tweaks. Interventions that target only the surface behaviour often fail because they do not address the deeper narrative. A budgeting app might track expenses, but if the underlying belief is "I'm bad with money," the individual may abandon the tool the first time they slip. What is needed is a reframing of identity itself. This can be achieved through incremental successes—small wins that contradict the dominant narrative—or through adopting new labels that align with aspirational change. Saying "I'm learning to manage money better" creates space for growth in a way "I'm terrible with money" never will.

The broader insight is that financial outcomes are shaped as much by identity as by income or knowledge. To the extent that people internalise their loops as unchangeable, they remain stuck in cycles of self-sabotage. To the extent they can see those loops as learned patterns rather than intrinsic truths, they can begin to shift them. *The moment a person stops saying "I'm bad with money" and starts saying "I've repeated unhelpful patterns, but I can learn new ones," the loop weakens.* Identity, then, is not a prison but a lens, and changing the lens changes the trajectory.

The transformation requires effort, patience, and often external support. But recognising how loops become identities is itself liberating. It reframes financial failure from an indictment of self to a consequence of repetition, habit, and narrative. In that reframing lies the possibility of change. The stories we tell ourselves about money are powerful, but they are not immutable. And once that is understood, the grip of destructive financial identities begins to loosen.

Chapter 6
The Hidden Logic of Saving and Spending

Few areas of human behaviour so vividly expose the tension between logic and instinct as the act of saving and spending. On the surface, these are financial choices: one either sets aside money for the future or uses it in the present. But beneath the surface lies a deeper psychological drama—one shaped by evolutionary biases, emotional triggers, and social conditioning. Why does saving, a decision most people recognise as rational and beneficial, often feel painful, even punitive? Why does spending, particularly on fleeting indulgences, deliver such immediate relief and pleasure, even when it undermines long-term goals? These questions point to a hidden logic—one not rooted in numbers but in psychology.

Neuroscience provides a crucial clue. The human brain evolved to prioritise short-term rewards over long-term security. In prehistoric environments, where food and resources were scarce, grabbing what was available immediately was adaptive. Delayed gratification, the cornerstone of saving, is a relatively modern demand, and the brain still perceives it as loss. Handing over money to a savings account, no matter how wise, triggers the same sense of sacrifice as parting with something essential. *Saving often feels like deprivation, not investment, because the reward is abstract, invisible, and deferred.* Spending, by contrast, activates the brain's reward circuitry instantly: the purchase, however trivial, delivers a tangible signal of satisfaction. The disparity between the two explains why even intelligent, financially literate individuals struggle to align their behaviours with their intentions.

Consider the phenomenon of the small indulgence: the takeaway coffee, the online impulse purchase, the upgrade to next-day delivery. From a purely financial standpoint, these are trivial amounts. Yet psychologically, they carry disproportionate weight. The minor purchase provides a sense of control, comfort, or identity affirmation that no long-term savings goal can replicate in the moment. This is why advice that frames these behaviours as wasteful—"give up your lattes and you'll be rich"—so often falls flat.

It misunderstands the emotional value embedded in small acts of spending. *The hidden logic of everyday indulgence is not about the item itself but about the relief, joy, or reassurance it provides.* To address this behaviour meaningfully, one must confront not just the arithmetic of costs but the emotional calculus of reward.

This dynamic also has a darker side, evident when saving itself becomes compulsive. Popular culture often portrays savers as virtuous, but extremes reveal another form of dysfunction. Some individuals hoard money obsessively, refusing to spend even when doing so would improve their well-being. Their accounts may be full, but their lives feel impoverished. Meals are skipped to avoid expense, opportunities are lost for fear of financial risk, generosity is withheld even when affordable. For these individuals, the act of saving is not an investment in the future but a shield against anxiety. The paradox is that their behaviour, though praised as responsible, can be as damaging as reckless spending. *An obsession with accumulation may protect against short-term insecurity but simultaneously erodes quality of life and relationships.*

The cultural dimension of saving and spending further complicates the picture. Societies lionise both the disciplined saver and the free spender, depending on context. Frugality is celebrated as prudence, yet lavish consumption is admired as success. The tension between these narratives creates confusion and guilt. One person feels ashamed for indulging, another feels ashamed for not living more fully, and both experience inner conflict. The hidden logic here is that money decisions are rarely about money alone; they are about identity, belonging, and meaning. Saving and spending are performed acts, signals to oneself and others about who one is and what one values. To reframe these behaviours requires recognising their symbolic as well as their practical dimensions.

Philosophically, the challenge is to reconcile present and future selves. The person who chooses to spend today is not irrational; they are prioritising the needs of the present self over the hypothetical well-being of a future self who may never arrive. Conversely, the compulsive saver over-invests in the future self at the expense of the present. Both positions miss the point that money is not solely a means of survival but a medium of experience. The deeper task is to redefine reward—not as immediate consumption or distant accumulation, but as the alignment of money with values. *The truest reward is not in the act of saving or spending itself, but in whether those acts serve a life that feels coherent, purposeful, and humane.*

Practical examples illustrate the power of reframing. A savings account labelled "freedom fund" feels different from one labelled "retirement account." The former connects saving with an emotionally resonant value—freedom, choice, autonomy—while the latter can feel abstract or punitive. Similarly, allowing for designated "joy spending" reframes indulgence not as weakness but as intentional living. In both cases, the individual is not fighting against the brain's reward system but enlisting it. Behavioural science has shown that when savings goals are linked to emotionally meaningful outcomes, people are more likely to persist, not because the mathematics changed but because the story did.

Modern technologies amplify both the problem and the solution. One-click purchases, subscription models, and algorithm-driven advertising exploit the brain's hunger for immediate gratification. Yet the same tools can be harnessed to encourage saving: apps that gamify deposits, visualise progress, or create micro-rewards when goals are met. These tools work not by changing the arithmetic of finance but by altering the emotional experience of saving. They reveal that the hidden logic of money is not about numbers on a screen but about the way those numbers are felt, interpreted, and woven into the fabric of daily life.

Ultimately, the hidden logic of saving and spending forces a re-examination of what money is for. If it exists solely to be hoarded, life becomes a rehearsal for a future that never arrives. If it exists solely to be spent, life becomes a series of fleeting highs followed by chronic instability. The balance lies in recognising that both saving and spending are emotional acts, and that true mastery comes from reframing them as tools to support a meaningful existence. By confronting the biases that make saving feel painful, by appreciating the allure of small rewards without being ruled by them, by acknowledging the dangers of compulsive accumulation, and by redefining what reward truly means, individuals can move beyond instinct and conditioning toward conscious choice. *The goal is not to suppress emotion but to understand it—to work with the hidden logic rather than against it.*

This chapter opens the door to that understanding. It asks the reader to look beneath the arithmetic of finance and into the psychology that shapes every financial decision. For within that psychology lies the possibility of transformation: a shift from unconscious loops of gratification and deprivation to a deliberate relationship with money that honours both present and future, indulgence and discipline, pleasure and purpose.

Why Saving Feels Painful

At first glance, saving money ought to be one of the simplest acts of financial prudence: setting aside today's surplus for tomorrow's needs. Yet for most people, saving feels less like a rational choice and more like an emotional sacrifice, a small wound that stings with every transfer into a savings account. The paradox is stark: even when individuals know that saving is beneficial, even when they acknowledge that their future self will thank them, they struggle to act in alignment with this knowledge. *The discomfort of saving is not rooted in arithmetic but in psychology, and specifically in the way the human brain processes reward and loss.*

The origins of this aversion to saving lie deep in evolutionary history. For our ancestors, survival hinged on immediate consumption. To see food and pass it by in the hope of eating later was to risk starvation. This ingrained bias for immediate gratification has endured into modern life, where the same cognitive machinery governs financial decision-making. Behavioural economists describe this tendency as *hyperbolic discounting*: the tendency to value immediate rewards disproportionately more than future ones. In practice, this means the pleasure of buying a meal, a gadget, or a holiday today outweighs the abstract promise of security decades down the line. Saving, therefore, is experienced not as gain but as loss—the loss of present comfort, enjoyment, or status.

This perception is reinforced by the way the brain encodes rewards. Neuroscientific research shows that dopamine, the neurotransmitter most closely associated with pleasure and motivation, spikes at the anticipation of a reward rather than its arrival. Spending, with its sensory immediacy—the smell of new leather, the glow of a screen displaying a purchase confirmation, the sight of a parcel at the door—provides rich triggers for the dopamine system. Saving, by contrast, offers no such sensory hook. A growing number in a digital account lacks the tangible cues that spark the brain's reward circuits. It is invisible, deferred, and uncertain. As a result, *spending feels like a victory, while saving feels like abstinence.*

This dynamic explains why even small expenditures can feel disproportionately satisfying. The "latte effect," much derided in personal finance commentary, misses the point. A coffee is not about caffeine; it is about the small ritual of indulgence, the immediate experience of treating oneself. Cutting out such purchases often feels like self-denial without an equivalent emotional replacement. Saving the cost of a latte does not deliver an immediate reward; the benefit is so distant and abstract that it rarely motivates behaviour. The brain does not naturally equate a foregone coffee today with a more comfortable retirement forty years hence. The logic is financial, but the lived experience is emotional.

There is also a cultural layer to this perception. Modern consumer societies condition individuals to see spending as a form of self-expression and social participation. Advertisements equate purchases with identity: one is not merely buying clothes but "expressing personality"; not merely buying a car but "fulfilling ambition." To save, therefore, is to forgo not just an item but a chance to signal belonging, achievement, or individuality. The cultural narrative equates accumulation of goods with the accumulation of meaning. Within this framework, saving appears as withdrawal, even invisibility, and thus carries subtle social penalties. *The pain of saving is intensified by the fear of missing out on the cultural currency of consumption.*

Interestingly, saving does not feel painful to everyone. Some individuals find comfort in the act, treating their growing balance as reassurance against uncertainty. Yet even for them, the satisfaction of saving is rarely immediate; it is cultivated by habit, reframed by meaning, or reinforced by social environment. For example, those raised in households where saving was celebrated as a marker of responsibility often experience it as positive rather than punitive. Others who frame savings accounts as "freedom funds" or "opportunity accounts" link the act to emotionally resonant values, transforming the pain of deprivation into the pleasure of empowerment. These exceptions confirm the rule: *saving feels painful unless its narrative is redefined.*

Psychological experiments underline this principle. In studies where participants were asked to choose between receiving a smaller amount of money now or a larger amount later, most opted for the smaller immediate gain—even when the larger reward was significantly higher. Yet when the delayed reward was reframed with emotional significance (for instance, presented as money for a future holiday or for family security), people were more likely to wait. The lesson is clear: the brain does not respond to abstract numbers but to stories and symbols. Reframing saving as an act of protection, empowerment, or self-respect alters its felt meaning.

Stress and uncertainty also magnify the difficulty of saving. When life feels precarious, immediate gratification becomes a coping mechanism. A purchase delivers not just pleasure but reassurance in the face of uncertainty. In such contexts, saving feels doubly painful because it requires withholding comfort in a moment of vulnerability. This is why advice to "just save more" often falls flat among those living with financial stress. The problem is not ignorance but the emotional calculus of survival. To save in the midst of insecurity is to deprive oneself of a vital psychological buffer. *The very times when saving is most needed are often the moments when it feels most impossible.*

There is, however, a philosophical counterpoint worth considering. If saving feels painful because it represents a sacrifice of the present self for the sake of the future self, then the challenge is to reconcile these two selves. The present self craves gratification; the future self demands security. Most people privilege the present because it is tangible, alive, and emotionally urgent. The future, by contrast, is an abstraction. Yet it is precisely this abstraction that allows saving to feel meaningful once it is anchored in a narrative of continuity. Framing saving as an act of care for one's future self—an extension of compassion across time—helps bridge the gap. In this way, saving becomes less about deprivation and more about self-respect, a recognition that the future self is no less real than the present one.

Technological innovations offer further strategies for reframing. Savings apps that gamify deposits, present visual progress, or allow micro-rewards create small dopamine hits that mimic the pleasure of spending. For instance, rounding up purchases and automatically transferring the difference into savings capitalises on existing spending behaviour while making saving effortless. Others use streaks, badges, or narratives that celebrate saving milestones, effectively transforming an act of abstinence into one of achievement. These tools reveal that saving feels painful only when it is divorced from the emotional architecture that governs human behaviour. When re-engineered to align with that architecture, saving can become not only tolerable but gratifying.

Ultimately, the pain of saving lies in a mismatch between rational understanding and emotional experience. Rationally, we know that saving is an investment in future well-being. Emotionally, it registers as a loss of pleasure, status, or identity in the present. To bridge this gap requires more than discipline; it requires a re-imagination of what saving means. Whether through cultural narratives, personal reframing, or technological tools, the challenge is to transform saving from a silent loss into a visible gain. *When saving is experienced not as deprivation but as empowerment, the pain subsides and the act becomes not only possible but rewarding in itself.*

This, then, is the hidden truth: saving feels painful not because it is unnatural but because it conflicts with instincts honed over millennia and cultural narratives crafted over decades. Yet once we acknowledge and understand this pain, we gain the power to reframe it—not as loss, but as an investment in the continuity of our own lives.

The Allure of Small Rewards

It is a curious feature of human psychology that a modest indulgence—a coffee from a favourite café, an impulsive online purchase, an evening takeaway—often delivers a more immediate sense of satisfaction than progress towards a long-term financial goal. Rationally, the numbers do not add up: the fleeting pleasure of a £4 coffee or a £20 purchase is trivial compared to the security of an emergency fund or the compounding effect of investment. Yet emotionally, the small indulgence is disproportionately rewarding, while the larger, delayed objective feels distant and abstract. *The human brain, primed for immediacy, elevates the trivial moment of gratification above the significant but deferred benefit.*

The disproportionate pull of these minor rewards is rooted in the same cognitive bias that makes saving feel like deprivation: the tendency to prioritise the present over the future. But the story runs deeper than simple impatience. Small rewards are alluring precisely because they are concrete, controllable, and instantly validating. Unlike long-term goals, which demand consistency over months or years, the satisfaction of a coffee, a new book, or a small gadget is achieved within minutes. The act is not only affordable but certain: no market volatility can erase the pleasure of an ice cream, and no distant timeline dilutes the feeling of opening a parcel. *The certainty of immediate indulgence often trumps the uncertainty of deferred outcomes.*

Neuroscience sheds further light on this dynamic. The brain's reward system responds most strongly to immediate, tangible cues. Dopamine release is not simply about the size of a reward but its proximity and salience. Thus, even minor pleasures create stronger neurological responses than abstract goals such as "retirement security" or "financial independence." These long-term aims, while rationally more valuable, lack the immediacy required to activate the brain's reward circuits with equal force. It is not surprising, then, that many individuals find themselves reaching repeatedly for low-cost indulgences while neglecting distant objectives.

The consumer economy has weaponised this tendency. Marketers understand that framing products as "treats" rather than necessities taps directly into the psychology of small rewards. From the advertising slogan that invites you to "treat yourself" to the loyalty card that gamifies repeat purchases, companies cultivate the association between consumption and emotional relief. Social media has amplified this by normalising daily indulgences as self-care rituals or lifestyle markers. In this environment, small rewards are not only tempting but socially sanctioned, presented as antidotes to stress or as expressions of individuality. *The allure of minor indulgence is reinforced by cultural narratives that equate consumption with comfort and care.*

The smallness of these rewards also disguises their cumulative weight. A single indulgence seems harmless, even wise, if it boosts morale after a difficult day. The problem emerges when this pattern repeats daily, quietly siphoning money away from long-term goals. This is not simply about arithmetic but about habit formation. Each indulgence strengthens the neural pathway that associates spending with relief or pleasure. Over time, the brain comes to expect these micro-rewards, much as it expects a morning coffee or an evening routine. The indulgence ceases to be an occasional luxury and becomes an unconscious ritual. In this way, *the allure of small rewards is less about their monetary cost than their capacity to embed themselves into identity and routine.*

Yet the phenomenon is not wholly negative. In some cases, small rewards serve as vital psychological scaffolding, preventing burnout or providing the motivation to persist with longer-term goals. For example, research on habit formation suggests that immediate reinforcement is essential for sustaining difficult behaviours. Someone saving for a house deposit may find it easier to stay disciplined if they allow themselves occasional small indulgences, reframed as conscious, budgeted rewards rather than unconscious leaks. The problem is not the indulgence itself but its unconsciousness: the slide from intentional reward to automatic reflex.

There is also a philosophical dimension to consider. If the small reward brings joy, is it truly irrational to prioritise it over a distant goal? Life is lived in the present, and long-term goals are often vulnerable to contingencies—health, employment, even mortality—that render them uncertain. To deny oneself every small indulgence in pursuit of a future that may never arrive is to risk an austere existence stripped of spontaneity and pleasure. Conversely, to pursue only immediate gratification is to risk future insecurity and regret. *The challenge lies not in eliminating small rewards but in integrating them consciously within a broader framework of financial and emotional well-being.*

One effective strategy is to reframe the long-term goal in terms that borrow from the immediacy of small rewards. For example, instead of viewing saving as an abstract contribution to a pension, it can be framed as a future "freedom purchase"—buying the option to leave a job earlier, to travel, or to support family members. By attaching emotional meaning and tangible imagery to the abstract, the long-term goal begins to compete more effectively with the pull of daily indulgences. Similarly, visualising progress—through charts, milestones, or gamified savings platforms—can provide the dopamine feedback usually reserved for small purchases.

Cultural and social context also matters. In environments where conspicuous consumption is normalised, small rewards often carry social validation. Sharing photos of meals, purchases, or experiences can convert a modest indulgence into a social signal of belonging or success. By contrast, saving is largely invisible, offering little recognition or reinforcement. This imbalance can be corrected when communities or peer groups celebrate financial discipline, making saving itself a socially validated act. Some financial literacy programmes have demonstrated success by fostering group challenges, where members publicly track savings milestones, transforming the invisible act of saving into a visible social achievement.

Crucially, small rewards need not always be monetary. Non-financial forms of indulgence—taking time for a walk, calling a friend, engaging in a hobby—can provide equal or greater psychological relief without eroding financial stability. Recognising this expands the menu of rewards beyond spending, reducing reliance on consumption as the default form of self-care. *The allure of small rewards need not be denied but redirected towards forms that enrich rather than deplete.*

What emerges from this exploration is a nuanced picture. The allure of small rewards is not a failure of willpower but a feature of human psychology, shaped by evolutionary pressures, neurological wiring, and cultural reinforcement. It explains why disciplined, intelligent individuals still find themselves succumbing to daily indulgences even when committed to larger goals. The answer is not to moralise against small rewards but to understand their function, to question their unconscious repetition, and to reframe the balance between immediate gratification and future security. *By making small rewards conscious and aligning them with long-term meaning, individuals can harness their power without being enslaved by them.*

The paradox remains: a small coffee or a minor purchase feels more satisfying in the moment than watching numbers in a savings account slowly rise. But understanding why this is the case—why the brain privileges immediacy, why culture validates indulgence, why habits form around minor pleasures—provides the first step toward rebalancing. The goal is not the elimination of small rewards but their rightful place in a life that honours both present joy and future stability.

When Saving Turns Toxic

The virtues of saving are so deeply ingrained in modern financial advice that questioning them can feel almost heretical. From childhood, people are told that thrift builds security, that restraint today ensures freedom tomorrow, and that a disciplined saver is morally superior to the reckless spender. Yet even virtues, when taken to an extreme, can become distortions. Saving, when driven not by prudence but by compulsion, can evolve into a quiet pathology—producing anxiety, deprivation, and isolation as corrosive as the debt-driven excess it seeks to avoid. *The paradox is that saving, often intended as a path to security, can become a prison that locks people away from life itself.*

At the heart of compulsive saving lies fear. For some, the fear is rational, born of scarcity in childhood or a direct encounter with financial instability. For others, it is less grounded in reality and more a chronic sense that no amount of money is ever "enough." The bank balance grows, but so too does the anxiety. What begins as sensible precaution—building a buffer against uncertainty—becomes an endless project of accumulation, where every purchase is scrutinised and every outflow feels like a threat to survival. *The saver is never reassured, because the behaviour is not about money but about managing fear.*

The psychological roots of such behaviour often mirror those of overspending. Just as some people use debt to mask insecurity or perform success, others use saving to control uncertainty or insulate themselves from imagined catastrophe. The compulsive saver derives identity and safety from hoarding, much as the compulsive spender derives them from display. Both patterns are driven by emotion rather than reason, and both can be destructive in their extremes. What distinguishes the compulsive saver is not financial discipline but rigidity: the inability to see money as a tool rather than an end in itself.

Case studies illustrate how saving can turn toxic. Consider the professional who lives in a modest home, avoids travel, and denies themselves leisure activities despite having ample resources. They tell themselves they are preparing for retirement or guarding against future risk, but in reality they are locked in a cycle where spending triggers acute guilt. Meals out are declined, holidays postponed, even small comforts rejected—not because they are unaffordable, but because they feel unjustifiable. Over decades, this leads not only to missed experiences but to strained relationships, as friends and family perceive the individual as joyless or withholding. The irony is sharp: in trying to protect their future, compulsive savers erode their present, and sometimes their social bonds too.

The culture of personal finance can inadvertently exacerbate this tendency. Financial gurus often promote extreme frugality as a badge of honour, celebrating stories of people who live on the bare minimum in order to amass impressive savings. While discipline and sacrifice have their place, these narratives can normalise unhealthy self-denial, framing it as virtue rather than compulsion. The individual who chooses never to travel, never to upgrade their living conditions, and never to indulge in life's pleasures is lauded for their thrift, even if the behaviour stems from anxiety rather than freedom. *The line between prudence and pathology is blurred when culture valorises sacrifice without examining motive or cost.*

The consequences extend beyond lifestyle. Research in behavioural economics shows that scarcity thinking—whether real or self-imposed—narrows cognitive bandwidth. A person who is constantly preoccupied with protecting their money may experience the same tunnel vision as someone burdened by debt, becoming risk-averse to the point of paralysis. Opportunities for growth, whether in career, investments, or personal development, are declined because they require spending. By refusing to invest in themselves or their environment, compulsive savers sometimes undermine the very security they seek. An untouched savings account may look robust, but it is a poor substitute for the compounding benefits of wise investment, professional advancement, or social capital built through generosity.

It is also worth recognising that saving, when toxic, is rarely about numbers alone. Two people with identical incomes and savings may experience entirely different emotional realities. One feels secure and enjoys a balanced life; the other feels constantly endangered and deprived. The difference lies not in the balance sheet but in the narratives they carry: one trusts that their resources are adequate, the other distrusts both their environment and their own ability to manage it. Compulsive saving, then, is best understood not as a financial problem but as a psychological one—an emotional stance towards uncertainty that manifests through money.

Yet, it would be simplistic to dismiss compulsive saving as wholly negative. In societies where overspending and debt are more visible problems, the saver's restraint can look enviable, even admirable. And for individuals who have survived true deprivation, the instinct to cling tightly to resources may be both understandable and adaptive. The problem arises when that instinct hardens into rigidity, cutting off not only unnecessary consumption but also life-enhancing experiences and acts of generosity. *The challenge is not to abandon saving but to cultivate flexibility—to know when holding back creates security and when it creates suffering.*

A balanced perspective requires reframing what saving is for. If money is stored only to accumulate, it risks becoming sterile. If it is stored to support life—security, freedom, experiences, relationships—it becomes purposeful. One practical shift is to distinguish between saving for "future needs" and saving for "future joy." The compulsive saver often focuses exclusively on the former, neglecting the latter. Allocating resources not only to emergencies and retirement but also to planned enjoyment can soften the rigidity.

A holiday fund, a gift budget, or even a "fun account" can transform saving from hoarding to enabling. In this way, spending becomes not a threat but an expression of financial strength.

Philosophically, compulsive saving reveals a tension at the heart of money itself: is its ultimate purpose to preserve or to enable? The compulsive saver answers with preservation, treating money as a shield against vulnerability. Yet this stance assumes that vulnerability can ever be eliminated, which is illusory. No sum of money can protect against every risk. Recognising this can be liberating: if money cannot erase uncertainty, then its role must be to balance security with the richness of lived experience. *A life of extreme saving may be financially secure but existentially impoverished.*

Ultimately, when saving turns toxic, it betrays the very principle that makes saving valuable: the capacity to expand options and create freedom. True financial health is not measured only by the size of an account but by the balance between security and fulfilment, between prudence and participation. Recognising when saving has crossed the line into compulsion is not easy, especially in cultures that equate frugality with virtue. But by examining the underlying emotions—fear, distrust, anxiety—and by reframing the purpose of money, individuals can restore balance. Saving can remain a source of strength, but only when it serves life rather than controls it.

Redefining Reward

Human beings are not purely rational actors making calculated trade-offs between consumption and saving. They are creatures wired for emotion, driven by the immediacy of sensation and the pull of psychological reward. The classic advice of "spend less, save more" often collapses in practice not because it is wrong but because it fails to account for how the brain interprets reward. The modern consumer's dilemma is not simply about resisting temptation but about reconciling an ancient neurological system—calibrated for survival in environments of scarcity—with the complex demands of long-term financial planning. If saving is perceived as deprivation while spending feels like a treat, the outcome is predictable: indulgence now wins over security later. To change behaviour, therefore, the meaning of reward must be rewritten. *Money habits shift not when rules are imposed but when the emotional calculus underpinning them is transformed.*

At its core, reward is a neurological process. Dopamine, the brain's anticipation chemical, is released not only when we acquire something but also in the moments leading up to acquisition. This explains why browsing shops, scrolling online catalogues, or even imagining a purchase can feel exciting. Saving, by contrast, lacks visible cues or immediate reinforcement. The numbers in a bank account grow silently; there is no sensory rush, no social validation, no short-term thrill. For many, setting aside £100 feels like losing £100 of present pleasure rather than gaining future security. Behavioural economists describe this as *present bias*: the tendency to value immediate rewards disproportionately over future ones. If the act of saving is coded in the brain as loss, the task becomes reframing it as gain.

One way this reframing occurs is through the creation of vivid future imagery. Studies show that when individuals are encouraged to visualise their future selves in detail—where they live, what they look like, what their daily lives involve—they are more likely to save. The abstract "retirement" or "future stability" becomes concrete and emotionally resonant. Instead of an anonymous account balance, saving is tied to a mental picture of comfort, freedom, or dignity. *The brain responds not to abstract principles but to vivid, emotionally charged scenarios.* For this reason, financial planners increasingly integrate exercises that help people anchor saving to personal narratives rather than generic goals.

Another effective approach is to introduce immediacy into saving itself. The rise of digital tools and fintech applications demonstrates how technology can provide feedback loops that make saving feel rewarding in the present. Apps that round up small purchases and transfer the difference into savings accounts create microbursts of achievement. Gamified systems that show progress in colourful charts or unlock "levels" of saving introduce a sense of accomplishment comparable to the satisfaction of crossing an item off a to-do list. These cues are not trivial gimmicks; they harness the same neurological machinery that makes spending gratifying, but they redirect it towards accumulation. The act of saving, once invisible, becomes visible and emotionally meaningful.

Crucially, redefining reward also requires addressing the cultural scripts that frame spending as celebratory and saving as joyless. Marketing has long tied consumption to life's milestones: birthdays, promotions, anniversaries, even mundane successes are framed as occasions to "treat yourself." By contrast, saving is rarely marketed as celebration. This imbalance means that many people turn instinctively to spending as a way to mark progress or alleviate stress. The challenge is to rebrand saving not as abstinence but as empowerment. Imagine if putting money aside were framed in cultural narratives as a sign of success equal to, or greater than, the purchase of a luxury item. A deposit into a savings account could be experienced as an act of self-congratulation: a message to oneself that "I am in control, I am building something, I am free."

Yet there is also danger in overcorrecting. Just as saving can turn toxic when compulsive, attempts to gamify or glorify frugality can slide into performative virtue. The point is not to glorify saving for its own sake but to align it with life's broader goals. For some, this means linking saving to generosity—recognising that money set aside today can fund meaningful gifts or charitable acts tomorrow. For others, it means connecting saving to adventure or freedom—knowing that each contribution to a fund represents one step closer to a desired experience. *The redefinition of reward must always return to the question: what is this money for?* Without purpose, saving risks becoming either joyless hoarding or fragile willpower against temptation.

An often-overlooked technique for reshaping reward is deliberate substitution. Rather than framing saving as an alternative to pleasure, individuals can identify low-cost or non-monetary sources of satisfaction that replace high-cost indulgences. The daily £5 coffee shop ritual, for instance, can be swapped for a weekly café outing framed as a treat, while the saved money is channelled into a visible, named fund—say, "holiday freedom" or "future home." In this way, the act of restraint does not feel like deprivation but like trading one kind of reward for another. The key lies in making the new reward emotionally salient, so the brain recognises it as a genuine gain.

Philosophically, redefining reward challenges the zero-sum mindset that dominates much of financial thinking—the assumption that spending and saving are locked in opposition. A richer perspective sees them as complementary expressions of value. Spending well is not failure; it is an act of aligning money with present values. Saving well is not sacrifice; it is an act of aligning money with future values. Both can be rewarding when approached with intention. The destructive pattern arises when spending is driven by impulse and saving by fear, leaving neither aligned with conscious purpose. By contrast, when both are framed as positive, intentional choices, the psychological burden eases.

Real-world examples illustrate the transformative potential of reframing. Consider the young professional who sets up a "travel fund" where each contribution is celebrated as an investment in future experiences rather than a denial of current pleasures. Or the couple who establish a ritual of reviewing savings goals together monthly, treating it as a joint achievement rather than a sterile chore. Over time, these practices build not only healthier finances but stronger identities—where being a saver is not about abstinence but about agency, and where spending becomes mindful rather than automatic.

The deeper insight is that money is never only about arithmetic; it is about meaning. If saving feels painful and spending feels rewarding, the imbalance is not in the numbers but in the stories we attach to them. By rewriting those stories—by making saving feel like achievement, by treating spending as deliberate expression rather than escape—individuals can rewire their financial lives at the emotional level where decisions are truly made. *The task is not to suppress the desire for reward but to expand its definition, so that both present joy and future freedom are celebrated as forms of wealth.*

In the end, the art of redefining reward is the art of integration. It is about bringing the immediacy of pleasure into harmony with the patience of planning, transforming saving from a source of tension into a source of pride, and spending from an act of impulse into an act of alignment. When this balance is achieved, money ceases to be a battleground between duty and desire. It becomes a language through which people affirm both who they are today and who they intend to become tomorrow.

Chapter 7
The Psychology of Debt

Debt is more than a ledger entry, more than an accumulation of interest rates and repayment schedules; it is a deeply psychological experience that shapes how individuals see themselves, how they relate to others, and how they interpret their place in society. Few financial instruments exert such a profound influence on identity. The weight of owing can press upon a person's sense of autonomy, recasting them from an agent of their own future into a subject beholden to an unseen creditor. To be in debt is not merely to face a financial burden but to carry an invisible mark—one that affects confidence, self-worth, and even moral self-perception. Debt has been called the defining economic condition of modern life, but its impact is as much emotional as economic. The chains may be invisible, yet their grip is real.

The language surrounding debt betrays its dual function as both financial and moral. Terms such as "liability," "obligation," and "arrears" carry undertones of failure, inadequacy, or even wrongdoing. Anthropologists have long noted that the idea of debt is bound to concepts of honour and duty; to be indebted is to be seen as incomplete, lacking, or even guilty. In modern contexts, this moral residue remains. People in debt often feel judged, not only by external institutions but by themselves. What begins as a pragmatic tool to access education, housing, or opportunity can mutate into a corrosive force that diminishes self-esteem and breeds secrecy. *Debt shapes identity, not simply balance sheets.*

One of the most insidious aspects of debt is the illusion of progress it can foster. Credit card companies, payday lenders, and refinancing firms encourage the ritual of minimum payments, offering borrowers a sense of control while ensuring their dependence. Each month, the act of paying a fraction of what is owed can feel like responsible action, yet the principal remains stubbornly intact, and interest accrues in the shadows. Refinancing, too, is marketed as liberation—a chance to "reset" or "consolidate"—but often it merely prolongs the cycle, extending repayment horizons and embedding individuals more firmly within the system. The psychology here is subtle: debt teaches people to equate motion with progress, even when they are running on a treadmill.

Avoidance compounds the problem. Many individuals respond to debt not with strategic planning but with psychological distancing. Bills are left unopened, bank statements go unread, and the full magnitude of the situation is quietly ignored. This is not mere negligence; it is a defence mechanism against shame. To confront debt directly can feel like confronting one's own inadequacy, and so denial becomes a refuge. Yet avoidance is costly. Interest compounds while the problem festers, transforming what might have been manageable into something overwhelming. *Debt thrives in the dark, nourished by secrecy and silence.* The paradox is that the very act of ignoring debt deepens its control, reinforcing the sense of helplessness that drove the avoidance in the first place.

The social dimension of debt cannot be overlooked. It infiltrates relationships, shaping dynamics of trust, dependency, and resentment. Couples often cite financial strain as one of the most corrosive forces in marriage, and debt lies at the heart of many of those conflicts. Hidden debts, once revealed, can rupture trust more sharply than infidelity. Within families, debt can become an intergenerational burden, with parents borrowing to support children's education or adult children assisting indebted parents. In workplaces, debt can determine career choices, pushing individuals towards higher-paying jobs they dislike or preventing them from taking entrepreneurial risks. On every level, the psychology of debt narrows horizons and constrains choices, not only in material terms but in terms of identity and freedom.

Breaking free from debt, therefore, requires more than financial restructuring. It demands a cognitive and behavioural shift—a reframing of debt not as a shameful secret but as a challenge to be confronted openly. Research in behavioural psychology suggests that small, visible wins are essential in reshaping the emotional experience of repayment. The "snowball method," where individuals pay off the smallest debts first regardless of interest rates, capitalises on the human preference for psychological reward over mathematical optimisation. Each cleared account provides a burst of motivation, turning progress from an abstract goal into a tangible reality. In this way, the narrative shifts: the individual begins to see themselves not as a debtor drowning in obligation but as an agent capable of incremental victory.

The cultural conversation surrounding debt must also evolve. Too often, the narrative casts borrowers as reckless, irresponsible, or morally deficient. In truth, debt is frequently a rational response to systemic pressures—housing markets that outpace wages, education systems that demand loans as entry fees, or health systems that turn misfortune into liability. By reframing debt as a structural challenge rather than a personal failing, individuals can disentangle their sense of self-worth from their financial circumstances. This shift matters: it enables people to approach repayment not as penance but as strategy, replacing shame with agency.

Yet there is a deeper philosophical point: to be free from debt is not simply to have zero balances but to reclaim one's psychological sovereignty. It is to live without the constant background hum of obligation, without the narrowing of possibility that debt enforces. To understand debt's psychology is to recognise that it is both a financial mechanism and a cultural narrative, both an economic burden and an emotional experience. And to master it requires more than spreadsheets—it requires courage, honesty, and the willingness to redefine one's relationship with money itself.

This chapter will therefore move beyond conventional advice to examine debt as a force that intertwines with identity, shapes relationships, and tests resilience. It will uncover how illusions of control keep borrowers trapped, how denial deepens the cycle, and how liberation begins not with numbers but with mindset. By the end, what will emerge is not simply a guide to debt management but a new way of seeing debt—as something that need not define, but can be confronted, understood, and ultimately transcended.

Debt as a Modern Bondage

Debt is sold as freedom: the freedom to study at a university one could not otherwise afford, the freedom to buy a home without waiting decades, the freedom to access healthcare, start a business, or simply smooth over the irregularities of income and expense that characterise everyday life. Yet for millions, this promise quickly reveals itself as a paradox. What begins as a tool of empowerment often becomes a form of servitude, shaping not just financial circumstances but identity, relationships, and one's very sense of dignity. The bondage of debt is not metaphorical hyperbole—it is a condition that restricts autonomy, narrows choices, and subtly dictates who people believe themselves to be.

The effects of debt stretch far beyond the mathematics of principal and interest. People seldom think of themselves as the sum of their bank balances, yet debt has a way of seeping into self-concept. To owe is to feel tethered; it is to wake with an obligation that quietly shadows every decision. Research shows that indebted individuals often internalise a sense of inadequacy, associating their financial condition with personal failure. *Debt, unlike many other financial states, is morally loaded—it implies mismanagement, overreach, or irresponsibility, even when the debt was incurred for survival rather than indulgence.* This stigma is powerful. It converts what should be a neutral financial mechanism into a source of shame, one that people carry silently into their relationships and daily interactions.

In intimate relationships, debt often acts as an invisible third partner. Couples in debt are more likely to experience conflict, secrecy, and mistrust. Studies have shown that hidden debts—whether a credit card balance concealed from a spouse or a payday loan taken in desperation—can devastate trust more completely than other forms of dishonesty. Conversations about money become fraught with defensiveness, blame, or avoidance, while decisions about the future are constrained by obligations to creditors. For some, debt dictates career choices: one partner may stay in a high-paying but unfulfilling role because the mortgage demands it; another may delay starting a family because of student loans. In such cases, debt is not simply a monthly payment but an organising principle of the relationship.

Socially, debt can create hierarchies and exclusions. Friends who gather for dinners, trips, or celebrations may not realise the hidden calculations of the indebted individual, who measures participation against mounting interest. The appearance of belonging often requires spending money one does not have, thereby reinforcing the cycle of debt. In cultures where financial success is equated with moral worth, debt becomes doubly punishing: not only does it strain resources, but it also positions individuals as lesser in the eyes of others. *To be in debt is to carry an unspoken mark that others rarely see but that the debtor feels constantly.* This is the essence of modern bondage: the restriction is invisible, yet its psychological weight is immense.

One of the most corrosive aspects of debt is the way it alters self-esteem. Debt creates a constant background hum of insufficiency. Even when an individual is competent, hardworking, and resourceful, the fact of owing can undermine their confidence. This is not irrational. The indebted person's choices are genuinely constrained—they cannot easily leave an unpleasant job, take risks, or pursue opportunities. But the psychological overlay exaggerates these constraints, convincing the individual that they are not merely temporarily limited but fundamentally incapable. Over time, people may adopt identities such as "I'm just bad with money" or "I'll never get ahead," which reinforce the very cycles they feel trapped in. *Debt does not merely reflect economic conditions; it sculpts the way people imagine themselves and their possibilities.*

Historically, the idea of debt has always been intertwined with notions of obligation and morality. Ancient civilisations often treated debt as a condition akin to slavery: those unable to pay might become bonded labourers or forfeit their families into servitude. Modern societies have abolished such practices, yet the psychological legacy persists. Today's debtor is not physically shackled, but the sense of being beholden to an institution, of working not for one's own future but to service an obligation, echoes these older patterns. The contemporary individual may be free to move, to choose employment, and to consume, but beneath this surface lies an enduring sense of captivity. *It is bondage not of the body but of the mind.*

The structural nature of debt complicates its personal toll. Many debts are not the result of recklessness but of systemic necessity. In the United States, for instance, student loans are often unavoidable for those seeking higher education. In countries without universal healthcare, medical debt can result from emergencies outside anyone's control. Mortgages, too, are framed as the rational path to security and homeownership, yet they lock individuals into decades of repayment. Recognising this structural element is vital, because the shame surrounding debt often blinds individuals to its systemic roots. By internalising blame, debtors absorb psychological punishment for conditions shaped by policy, markets, and culture. The bondage is intensified not just by the financial obligation but by the narrative that they alone are at fault.

Yet it would be simplistic to portray debt only as oppression. For some, debt is a strategic tool that enables upward mobility, allowing access to education, homes, or businesses that would otherwise be impossible. The bondage arises not in the existence of debt but in its persistence, in the way it becomes inescapable and identity-defining. The distinction lies between using debt temporarily as leverage and living perpetually under its shadow. In modern economies, however, the line between these states is thin. Refinancing, minimum payments, and easy credit blur the boundary, making it difficult for individuals to ever truly escape. *The freedom promised by debt is often an illusion, carefully structured to ensure ongoing dependence.*

The question, then, is how individuals can recognise and resist the identity-shaping force of debt. The first step is psychological: to separate one's sense of self from one's financial obligations. This does not eliminate the practical challenges of repayment, but it prevents the corrosive fusion of debt with shame. The second step is relational: to bring debt out of secrecy. When debts are acknowledged openly—whether within families, couples, or communities—they lose part of their power. Finally, the cultural narrative must be confronted. As long as societies equate financial indebtedness with personal failure, debt will continue to operate as bondage. But by reframing it as a structural condition, shaped as much by economic systems as by individual choices, the stigma can be reduced and the path to freedom clarified.

Debt as a modern bondage is not only an economic reality but a psychological and cultural one. It binds individuals not simply by contracts but by identities, not only by repayment schedules but by relationships. To understand debt in this deeper sense is to see it not as a private misfortune but as a defining feature of contemporary life. And it is only by recognising this hidden dimension that individuals can begin to loosen its grip—not just by paying down balances but by reclaiming their sense of autonomy, dignity, and worth.

The Illusion of Control

Few financial habits feel more reassuring than making a payment. The act itself suggests movement: money is leaving the account, a balance is shrinking, progress is being made. Yet, for millions who make only the minimum payments on credit cards, or who repeatedly refinance debts into new arrangements, this sense of progress is a mirage. What appears as control is often the deepening of dependency. The structures of consumer finance are designed to provide precisely this illusion—a psychological balm that quiets anxiety without fundamentally reducing the burden.

Credit card minimum payments epitomise this deception. By design, they are calculated to be just low enough to keep repayment stretched over years, even decades, generating extraordinary profits for lenders. A balance of a few thousand pounds, paid only at the minimum each month, can cost multiples of its original amount once interest accumulates. Yet the psychological effect of sending in that small amount is soothing. *It feels like action, like responsible participation, when in truth it is the maintenance of stasis.* The borrower, reassured by the act of paying, delays confronting the scale of the problem. The creditor, meanwhile, benefits from an indefinite revenue stream.

Refinancing plays a similar role, albeit in more sophisticated form. The language of refinancing—resetting terms, reducing interest rates, consolidating obligations—promises clarity and relief. For some, when used strategically, it can indeed reduce costs or provide breathing space. But too often it functions as a reset button that extends indebtedness. Mortgages are refinanced to stretch thirty years of payments into forty; credit card balances are consolidated into loans that free up available credit, which is then spent again. The result is not escape but entrenchment: the appearance of a new start conceals the reality of deepened dependence. *Refinancing pacifies immediate discomfort while embedding long-term vulnerability.*

The attraction of these mechanisms lies in the way they manipulate human psychology. Behavioural economics has demonstrated that people are highly sensitive to immediate relief but discount future costs. To pay a minimum feels like satisfying an obligation today, even if it guarantees greater costs tomorrow. To refinance feels like wiping the slate clean, even though the slate has merely been re-etched in finer print. This disconnect is amplified by financial institutions, which deliberately frame repayment options in ways that maximise psychological comfort while preserving profitability. The illusion of control is therefore not accidental—it is engineered.

Consider the credit card statement. The most prominent figure displayed is often the minimum payment due, not the total balance or the projected interest costs. This framing steers attention to the smallest, easiest figure, nudging the borrower towards the path of least resistance. Similarly, refinancing is marketed with language of empowerment: "Take control of your debt," "Simplify your payments," "Unlock savings." Rarely do advertisements emphasise the long-term cost of prolonging repayment. *Control is presented as a matter of convenience and short-term ease rather than true reduction of obligations.*

The harm of this illusion extends beyond numbers. Psychologically, it allows individuals to preserve a self-image of responsibility while remaining ensnared. People who make minimum payments tell themselves they are "keeping up." Those who refinance frame the act as "smart financial management." In reality, the underlying debt remains, often larger or more enduring than before. The gap between perception and reality widens until a reckoning becomes unavoidable. At that point, shame intensifies: the individual feels not only the weight of debt but also the humiliation of having believed themselves in control.

This phenomenon also shapes social and cultural narratives about money. Many societies valorise the appearance of financial discipline—making payments on time, refinancing strategically, keeping up with bills. Less attention is paid to whether these behaviours actually reduce debt or build wealth. Thus, the illusion of control becomes a form of social camouflage. A household may outwardly seem responsible, even prosperous, while internally living on the edge of insolvency. Friends and colleagues may applaud the purchase of a refinanced home or a new car acquired through extended credit, without recognising that such moves entrench obligations rather than free the household from them.

The tension here is subtle but profound: *people crave both relief and progress, yet the structures of consumer finance often force them to choose one at the expense of the other.* Minimum payments and refinancing deliver relief, but not progress. Genuine progress—aggressively reducing principal, resisting re-borrowing—requires discomfort, discipline, and sacrifice. The illusion thrives because it offers a way to avoid that discomfort, even as it delays genuine resolution.

Critically, the illusion of control is not confined to the financially naïve. Highly educated, financially literate individuals fall prey to it as well. The pressures of modern life—housing costs, medical expenses, student loans—can make refinancing or making minimum payments seem not only rational but necessary. In such contexts, the illusion is less about ignorance and more about survival. Yet this distinction does not lessen the eventual cost. Dependency deepens regardless of intention, and the longer it persists, the harder it becomes to reverse.

Breaking the illusion requires a shift in perspective. It demands that individuals measure control not by the act of making a payment but by the trajectory of the balance itself. Real control means reducing obligations, not maintaining them at manageable levels. It also means recognising the structural forces at play: lenders are not neutral facilitators but active engineers of dependency. To see through the illusion is to reclaim a measure of autonomy, even if the practical path forward remains arduous.

The minimum payment and the refinanced loan are not, in themselves, inherently destructive. In certain contexts—temporary hardship, carefully planned debt restructuring—they can be pragmatic tools. The danger lies in the comfort they provide, the false reassurance that something meaningful has been achieved. *The illusion of control is powerful precisely because it is partial: it contains just enough truth to mask the deeper reality.* It is this half-truth, sustained month after month, year after year, that transforms manageable obligations into lifelong captivity.

Debt, then, is not merely a financial state but a psychological battleground. The illusion of control is one of its most effective weapons, keeping people docile, hopeful, and compliant while their dependency quietly grows. To expose this illusion is not simply to warn against financial products; it is to challenge the very narratives of responsibility and progress that underpin contemporary consumer life. Only by recognising the illusion for what it is can individuals move from the appearance of control to its reality—a state defined not by payments made but by obligations diminished, and by the restoration of genuine financial freedom.

Debt Denial and Avoidance

Debt is rarely a purely financial matter. It is equally, and often more powerfully, an emotional burden. While the numbers on a statement may be clear, the psychological weight they carry is less easily faced. This is why so many people, even the educated and outwardly disciplined, slip into patterns of denial and avoidance when it comes to their obligations. Instead of confronting the problem directly, they minimise its severity, delay opening bills, or convince themselves that everything will resolve "eventually." The short-term relief provided by avoidance is potent, but it comes at the cost of long-term entrapment. *Debt is not simply carried in the bank account; it is carried in the mind, and the mind has ingenious ways of postponing pain.*

One of the most common strategies is selective attention. People in debt often engage in what psychologists call attentional bias, focusing on financial information that feels manageable while ignoring that which feels overwhelming. A credit card with a small balance may be paid diligently, while the larger, higher-interest account is neglected. Opening one bill becomes a token of responsibility, a way to soothe anxiety, while other envelopes remain unopened in a drawer. In this way, individuals maintain the illusion of engagement while avoiding the aspects of their debt that most demand attention.

Another form of denial is reframing debt as temporary or exceptional. Borrowers often tell themselves, "This is just a rough patch," or, "Once the bonus arrives, everything will be fine." While sometimes true, these reframings can persist for years, with each new expense rationalised as an exception. This mindset delays corrective action because it portrays debt not as a chronic condition requiring structural change, but as a passing inconvenience. *The debt itself becomes invisible, disguised beneath the story that life is about to improve.*

Emotional avoidance also manifests in procrastination. Bills are left unopened not because the person cannot physically open them, but because doing so forces them to confront their anxiety. The act of not looking creates a temporary sense of safety. Unfortunately, debt thrives in silence. Interest accumulates, penalties grow, and options narrow with each month of avoidance. What feels protective in the moment becomes destructive over time. This pattern mirrors other avoidance behaviours seen in human psychology: from avoiding medical check-ups to ignoring relationship conflicts, people often choose short-term emotional comfort over long-term well-being. With debt, the costs of this comfort compound relentlessly.

Denial also plays out socially. Many individuals conceal the extent of their debt from family, friends, or partners. Some downplay it—"I've just got a bit on the cards"—while others avoid the subject entirely. This secrecy isolates them further, depriving them of potential support and reinforcing the cycle of shame. *Debt becomes not only a financial liability but a private identity crisis, something to be hidden at all costs.* The paradox is that by avoiding disclosure, individuals often make decisions that deepen the very burden they are trying to conceal, such as taking out additional loans in secret or continuing consumption patterns that sustain appearances.

At a deeper level, denial and avoidance reveal the human brain's difficulty with abstract future costs. Neurological research shows that people experience debt stress not as a rational calculation of future interest but as an immediate emotional threat. The mind seeks to alleviate this threat through avoidance, not by solving the underlying problem. It is why some people will continue spending as though nothing is wrong, seeking the fleeting comfort of consumption while burying their awareness of looming obligations.

The very behaviour that created the debt becomes the mechanism for numbing its consequences.

This dynamic can be seen in the rise of "buy now, pay later" schemes, which are marketed as painless ways to spread costs. For many, these arrangements normalise denial by making obligations invisible. The payment is pushed into the future, beyond the horizon of current concern, allowing the individual to enjoy the purchase without confronting its cost. Over time, these micro-deferrals accumulate into a web of commitments that feel unmanageable only when it is too late to undo them.

The tragedy of denial and avoidance is that they often lead to moments of crisis. The unopened bills eventually lead to default notices; the concealed debts eventually come to light in relationships; the small rationalisations build until bankruptcy or repossession becomes unavoidable. By the time the individual confronts reality, options are fewer and the emotional toll is heavier. This is why financial counsellors emphasise early intervention: *debt unacknowledged is debt magnified.*

Yet it is important to recognise that denial is not mere irresponsibility. It is, at its core, a coping mechanism. People avoid debt because they fear what it says about them. In cultures where financial success is equated with self-worth, to acknowledge unmanageable debt feels like admitting personal failure. Thus, denial protects not just from numbers but from shame. The irony is that this protection erodes dignity further, as the avoidance inevitably leads to worse outcomes than honesty and action might have achieved.

Breaking the cycle of denial requires both emotional and cognitive shifts. On the emotional side, individuals must decouple debt from identity, recognising it as a circumstance rather than a reflection of character. On the cognitive side, they must reframe avoidance as a danger, not a shield. Behavioural strategies—such as automatic payments, accountability with a trusted friend, or confronting balances daily—can help weaken the tendency to look away. The act of facing numbers consistently, however uncomfortable, gradually restores agency.

Ultimately, the struggle against debt denial and avoidance is not just about financial management but about confronting the human instinct to protect oneself from pain. To look away feels easier, but it also allows the problem to grow. To look directly at debt, with clarity and without self-condemnation, is an act of courage. It replaces the fragile comfort of avoidance with the sturdier foundation of reality. *Only by replacing denial with acknowledgment can individuals begin the work of transforming debt from an unspoken shadow into a challenge that can be managed, confronted, and eventually overcome.*

Breaking Free

Freedom from debt is not only a matter of numbers on a balance sheet; it is a psychological and behavioural transformation. Many people labour under the assumption that the technical solution—a higher-paying job, a debt consolidation loan, or a stricter budget—is sufficient. Yet the history of personal finance shows otherwise: without addressing the cognitive and emotional scripts that sustain indebtedness, even substantial increases in income or favourable repayment arrangements often fail to bring lasting change. *To break free from debt is to break free from the mental and behavioural loops that make debt feel inevitable.*

One of the most important shifts is learning to separate shame from responsibility. Debt often carries moral weight in society, and those who find themselves overwhelmed may internalise narratives of failure: "I am bad with money" or "I lack self-control." This self-condemnation not only obscures the structural realities that often shape debt—such as aggressive lending practices, rising costs of living, or stagnant wages—but also paralyses action. When shame dominates, individuals are more likely to avoid confronting their finances, leaving them trapped in the very cycles they wish to escape. The first step towards freedom is therefore cognitive: *to see debt not as a verdict on character but as a solvable circumstance.* Responsibility must replace shame, because responsibility is empowering—it recognises both the part one has played and the power one has to change course.

Behavioural shifts are equally vital. Research in behavioural economics has shown that human beings are wired to prefer immediate relief over long-term gain, a bias that makes debt repayment particularly difficult. Minimum payments on credit cards, for instance, feel easier because they reduce immediate anxiety, even though they extend the debt horizon indefinitely. To counter this bias, individuals can restructure repayment behaviour by creating immediate, visible markers of progress. Techniques such as the "debt snowball"—focusing repayment efforts on one balance at a time, while maintaining minimums on others—work not only because of the mathematics of interest reduction, but because they provide a psychological win. *Freedom requires designing behaviours that exploit, rather than fight against, the quirks of human motivation.*

Another crucial dimension is reframing the narrative around consumption. Many indebted individuals remain caught in cultural scripts that equate spending with worth or belonging. To break free, one must challenge these scripts head-on. Instead of asking, "Can I afford this?"—a question that often leads to rationalisations—people can ask, "Does this purchase support the life I want to build?" This reframing introduces intentionality into decisions, shifting spending from an automatic reflex to a conscious choice aligned with values. Over time, this shift reshapes identity: the person moves from being a passive consumer to being an active curator of their financial and personal life.

Facing debt also requires dismantling avoidance behaviours. As discussed previously, many people fall into denial—ignoring bills, underestimating balances, or hiding obligations from themselves and others. Breaking free demands the opposite: radical clarity. This can take the form of regular financial check-ins, accountability with a trusted partner, or even confronting balances daily until they no longer induce panic. Though uncomfortable, the practice of facing the numbers strips them of their power. *Avoidance breeds helplessness; confrontation breeds agency.*

Equally significant is the recognition that debt management is not a solitary endeavour. Cultural narratives often frame money as a private matter, but secrecy perpetuates shame and weakens resilience. Seeking support—whether from financial counsellors, peer groups, or even trusted friends—can provide both practical advice and psychological relief. Social accountability interrupts isolation, and collective wisdom often reveals paths forward that individuals cannot see on their own. The very act of disclosure, of speaking openly about debt, can be liberating: it transforms an internalised burden into a shared problem that can be addressed.

Breaking free also means learning to replace destructive coping mechanisms with healthier ones. Many fall into debt because spending temporarily alleviates stress or provides a sense of control in otherwise uncontrollable lives. If the underlying emotional needs remain unaddressed, repayment alone will not sustain change. Cognitive-behavioural approaches encourage individuals to identify the emotional triggers for spending—boredom, loneliness, status anxiety—and replace the associated behaviours with alternatives that meet those needs without financial damage. A walk, a conversation, or a creative project may not deliver the same instant dopamine hit as a purchase, but over time, these alternatives create more stable sources of fulfilment. *Freedom is not achieved by removing the need for comfort, but by finding comfort that does not cost tomorrow's security.*

Importantly, the process of breaking free must also account for identity. Many individuals carry internalised labels such as "I'm terrible with money," which act as self-fulfilling prophecies. Each poor decision reinforces the belief, and the belief in turn justifies further poor decisions. To escape this loop, one must consciously cultivate a new financial identity. Small shifts—such as calling oneself "a learner with money" or "a disciplined steward"—gradually reshape self-perception. Behaviour follows belief, and when identity aligns with financial health, sustaining positive change becomes easier.

Finally, breaking free involves a long-term redefinition of what financial freedom means. Too often, people set unrealistic goals of total transformation—becoming debt-free overnight, or living with absolute austerity. These ambitions, while well-intentioned, can lead to discouragement when progress is slow. Instead, freedom can be understood as incremental: each step towards reduced dependency, each habit that sustains clarity, each decision that prioritises future security is a form of liberation. The shift from debt as bondage to debt as manageable obligation begins with perspective. By viewing progress as a series of compounding victories rather than an all-or-nothing event, individuals build resilience and momentum.

Breaking free from debt, then, is not a single action but a constellation of shifts—cognitive, behavioural, emotional, and social. It requires courage to confront shame, intentionality to reshape spending, strategies that align with human psychology, and support that interrupts isolation. Above all, it demands a reimagining of self: from debtor to decision-maker, from consumer to creator, from captive to free. *Debt may begin as a financial condition, but freedom from it is a transformation of mind and identity. It is not simply the absence of obligation, but the presence of agency and possibility.*

Chapter 8
Money and Identity

Few forces shape our relationship with money more profoundly than the question of identity. Beneath every purchase, investment, or financial decision lies an often-unspoken dialogue about who we believe ourselves to be, who we wish to become, and how we want others to perceive us. Unlike the arithmetic of income and expenses, identity is not easily itemised or balanced; it is embedded in social expectations, cultural narratives, and personal histories. Money serves as both a mirror and a mask—reflecting our sense of worth while concealing our insecurities. To understand money without examining identity is to miss the very foundation upon which financial behaviour rests.

Consider the way individuals spend not simply to acquire goods but to signal belonging. Identity groups—whether class, race, profession, or religion—carry their own financial codes, sometimes explicit, often unspoken. A young professional entering the corporate world may feel compelled to purchase tailored suits not merely for practicality but as proof of competence and assimilation. A family within a religious community may prioritise donations, rituals, or symbols of devotion, even if doing so strains their budget, because such spending affirms membership in something larger than themselves. Class markers are especially persistent: handbags, watches, cars, and even holiday destinations serve as shorthand for where one "belongs" in the social order. *Spending, in these cases, is rarely about the intrinsic utility of the object; it is about reinforcing identity and securing acceptance.*

Yet belonging is only one dimension. Money also carries enormous weight as a proxy for self-worth. In cultures where success is measured by financial achievement, income and net worth become entangled with personal value. A bonus at work does not just increase bank balances; it elevates self-esteem. Conversely, financial setbacks—redundancy, debt, or stagnation—can provoke a crisis of identity, leaving individuals questioning not only their economic security but their very worthiness. This psychological entanglement is especially visible in professions where performance is quantified—

sales targets, quarterly earnings, or investment returns. The fluctuation of numbers becomes a fluctuation of self. For many, this link is so entrenched that separating self-worth from financial worth feels nearly impossible. *Money does not simply measure what we have; it is used, dangerously, to measure who we are.*

Identity is also shaped by the labels society assigns. To be "rich" or "poor" is not merely to occupy a financial position; it is to carry an identity that informs expectations, aspirations, and behaviours. Those who internalise a "poor" identity may begin to see financial advancement as beyond their reach, reinforcing cycles of limitation. They may hear phrases such as "people like us can't afford that" or "we've never been good with money," and gradually accept them as truths. Likewise, those who grow into a "rich" identity may feel pressure to constantly prove and maintain it, even at the expense of genuine security. These identities act as invisible boundaries: a person may unconsciously sabotage opportunities for improvement because success would conflict with their entrenched self-image. The most insidious aspect of these labels is not their external application but their internalisation—when the story society tells becomes the story one tells oneself.

The path forward lies in recognising that money identity is not fixed but chosen. While early environments, cultural contexts, and inherited narratives exert powerful influence, they do not dictate destiny. By examining the scripts that shape financial identity, individuals can begin to separate authentic values from imposed expectations. Choosing a new identity might mean redefining what success looks like—not as the accumulation of status symbols, but as autonomy, security, or the freedom to pursue meaningful work. It might involve rejecting inherited scripts of scarcity or entitlement, instead cultivating a sense of stewardship and intentionality. Crucially, this redefinition requires disentangling self-worth from external comparison. *The healthiest money identities are those anchored not in status but in values, not in labels but in autonomy.*

This chapter will illuminate how identity groups shape spending, why financial worth is so often conflated with personal worth, and how labels of "rich" and "poor" entrap individuals in limiting beliefs. More importantly, it will show that financial identity is malleable. By questioning the scripts we inherit and consciously choosing the identities we inhabit, we can reshape our relationship with money in ways that support both psychological well-being and financial resilience. The exploration of money and identity is not peripheral to financial literacy; it is its essence. To understand who we are in relation to money is to unlock the possibility of not only better financial choices, but a freer and more authentic life.

Spending to Belong

Human beings are not only economic actors but deeply social creatures, and our relationship with money reflects this truth more vividly than almost any other domain. Spending decisions are rarely the outcome of solitary logic; they are embedded in the desire to connect, to affiliate, and to signal membership within identity groups that define us. Whether by class, race, profession, or religion, the groups we belong to exert a subtle yet persistent influence over how we use money—not merely as a tool of transaction, but as a marker of belonging. The drive to spend in alignment with group norms is not frivolous; it is one of the most powerful, and costly, forces shaping financial behaviour.

Consider class identity. The cues of belonging to a particular class are often embedded in the smallest and most mundane spending choices. The middle-class professional who purchases organic produce and prioritises private education is affirming more than nutritional or academic standards; they are signalling membership in a cultural group defined by values of health, achievement, and aspiration. The working-class family that invests in branded trainers or high-end electronics, even when budgets are tight, may be performing a different but equally potent form of belonging: affirming dignity, style, and resistance to invisibility. These purchases are not irrational when understood as symbolic investments in identity, though they can be financially perilous. *To spend in line with class expectations is to purchase not only an object but also a place in a story about who one is and where one fits.*

Race and ethnicity add another layer to the calculus of spending. Minority groups, particularly in societies where economic inequality and discrimination are structural, often use consumption to assert presence and counter narratives of exclusion. A Black professional in Britain may feel compelled to dress impeccably or drive a prestigious car, not solely for personal enjoyment but as an armour against the prejudices that question competence or legitimacy. In immigrant communities, collective spending on weddings, funerals, or remittances to family abroad functions as a moral obligation, binding individuals to networks of loyalty and belonging. These practices are not simply habits; they are acts of identity maintenance in the face of historical marginalisation or cultural dislocation. *Spending, in these contexts, is a way of asserting: we exist, we contribute, we belong.*

Professions, too, create their own economies of belonging. Lawyers, bankers, and consultants are expected to wear tailored suits, dine in specific establishments, and display markers of success consistent with their industry. Creative professionals, on the other hand, may be expected to adopt a cultivated nonchalance—investing in experiences, aesthetics, or avant-garde tastes that distinguish them from the corporate mainstream. Even within academia, where status is ostensibly tied to intellectual merit, material signals—attendance at international conferences, the books one cites, or the technology one carries—become subtle markers of group identity. Money in these cases becomes an unspoken language, signalling seriousness, competence, or authenticity in ways words alone cannot achieve.

Religion and spiritual communities provide some of the most enduring examples of identity-driven spending. Tithes, offerings, donations, and financial contributions to shared rituals are not merely economic sacrifices; they are acts of faith and belonging. A devout member of a congregation who gives beyond their means may be motivated less by abstract theology than by the desire to remain integrated in the community's moral and social fabric. In Islamic contexts, the practice of zakat (almsgiving) is not optional but foundational, reinforcing both religious identity and social solidarity. In other traditions, conspicuous spending on festivals or rituals may serve as proof of devotion and commitment. *Here, money functions not as a private asset but as a communal signal: to spend is to be seen, to contribute is to belong.*

The mechanisms behind these behaviours are both psychological and sociological. Social identity theory suggests that individuals derive part of their self-concept from group membership, and financial behaviours are one of the most visible ways of affirming that membership. Spending is a public act; it leaves traces that can be observed, interpreted, and judged. Choosing not to spend in alignment with group norms often carries social penalties, ranging from subtle exclusion to outright ostracism. This creates a paradox: individuals may prioritise short-term group acceptance over long-term financial stability, willingly undermining personal economic security for the sake of maintaining identity coherence. *The cost of non-conformity can feel greater than the cost of debt.*

Yet the pressure to spend to belong is not monolithic; it varies across cultures, generations, and economic contexts. In collectivist societies, communal obligations often outweigh personal financial preferences, while in individualist cultures the performance of uniqueness may itself become a form of conformity, leading to spending patterns that emphasise distinction. The rise of digital communities has further complicated this landscape. Social media enables the formation of virtual identity groups where belonging is maintained through curated consumption—whether through shared aesthetics on Instagram, collective investments in cryptocurrency, or participation in consumer subcultures. The boundaries of belonging are now policed not only in physical communities but also in algorithmically mediated digital spaces.

Philosophically, the phenomenon raises uncomfortable questions about autonomy. If spending is so deeply tied to identity, to what extent are financial decisions ever truly individual? Can one claim to be financially independent when one's consumption patterns are governed by the need to maintain group membership? This tension between autonomy and belonging lies at the heart of financial behaviour. The desire for authenticity clashes with the need for connection, producing spending habits that may seem contradictory but are, in fact, deeply human.

Practical implications of this dynamic are significant. Understanding that spending is often about identity rather than utility can reframe financial planning. Advisers who treat overspending as mere irrationality miss the deeper logic: people are not buying goods, they are buying belonging. Interventions that fail to address identity pressures are likely to fall flat. For example, telling a young adult to abandon branded clothing in favour of generic alternatives ignores the fact that those clothes serve as entry tickets to peer acceptance. A more effective approach might involve exploring alternative forms of belonging that are less financially costly. *To change spending habits, one must often first change the narratives of identity that underpin them.*

There are, of course, ways to resist these pressures. Some individuals deliberately opt out of group spending expectations, embracing frugality as a countercultural identity in itself. Movements such as minimalism, voluntary simplicity, or the FIRE (Financial Independence, Retire Early) community reframe belonging around non-consumption, creating counter-narratives where identity is signalled not by what is bought but by what is refused. These examples illustrate that spending to belong is not inevitable; it is a social script that can be rewritten. However, opting out requires courage, as it often entails reconfiguring one's social networks and redefining sources of self-worth.

Ultimately, spending to belong reveals both the promise and peril of money's social role. On one hand, it strengthens bonds, fosters community, and enables shared identity. On the other, it can trap individuals in cycles of spending that compromise long-term stability. The challenge lies in recognising when money is being used as a tool of connection and when it has become a chain of obligation. By making the implicit visible, individuals can begin to exercise greater choice, reshaping their financial lives not by rejecting belonging but by redefining the terms under which they seek it.

To spend is to belong, but belonging does not have to be purchased at the cost of freedom. When individuals understand the pressures that shape their financial choices, they can begin to belong on their own terms—anchored in values, not dictated by the price tags of conformity.

Money as Self-Worth

Few forces shape self-esteem as powerfully as money. While people may profess that character, kindness, or creativity matter most, the reality is that in many societies wealth has become shorthand for value. Net worth is often confused with self-worth, and financial performance functions as a visible scoreboard in the silent competition of life. This conflation is not accidental but deeply rooted in cultural narratives, economic structures, and psychological vulnerabilities that make wealth an alluring yet dangerous proxy for personal value.

The roots of this entanglement stretch back centuries. In capitalist societies, productivity and prosperity have long been held up as indicators of moral virtue. The Protestant work ethic, particularly influential in Western cultures, equated diligence and financial success with spiritual righteousness. While secularisation has diluted the religious framing, the underlying logic persists: wealth suggests discipline, competence, and superiority; poverty implies failure, laziness, or lack of control. Such narratives remain powerful even when discredited by evidence of systemic inequality, generational disadvantage, and sheer luck. *The judgement lingers not only externally, but internally: many evaluate their own worth by the size of their bank account.*

At the psychological level, money provides a seductive clarity that self-esteem often lacks. Self-worth is intangible and prone to fluctuation, but money offers a number, a measurable benchmark that can be compared, tracked, and displayed. Salaries, savings, and assets become the raw materials for a personal scoreboard. The annual bonus is not merely income; it is confirmation of competence and recognition of value. Conversely, redundancy or financial strain can feel like existential diminishment. This explains why the loss of wealth is often experienced as a crisis of identity rather than simply a practical problem. The collapse of a business, the foreclosure of a home, or even the decline of a retirement fund can shake the foundations of a person's self-concept, leaving scars long after financial recovery has taken place.

Modern consumer culture intensifies this link between money and self-worth. Advertising does not simply promote products; it promotes identities. Luxury brands in particular sell more than goods—they sell validation. A designer watch or handbag functions as a wearable declaration of significance: *I am successful, I matter, I belong among the accomplished.* Even non-luxury items carry status cues, as algorithms feed consumers with images of lifestyles to which they are meant to aspire. In this way, the marketplace actively trains individuals to externalise their self-worth, relocating it from the inner world of values to the outer world of possessions.

This dynamic is visible in professional life as well. Career achievements are measured not only in titles but in earnings. The corporate associate who resents their modest salary in comparison to peers is not simply concerned about material comfort but about perceived value: a smaller paycheck feels like a smaller self. Entrepreneurs, too, often conflate the success of their ventures with their own worth, making failure intolerable and driving risky behaviour in pursuit of validation. *When money is bound to esteem, financial setbacks become personal humiliations, and prudent caution is easily sacrificed for the chance of redemption.*

Cultural contrasts illuminate both the universality and variability of this pattern. In collectivist cultures, worth may be tied less to individual wealth than to one's ability to provide for family or community, yet money remains central as the mechanism for fulfilling those duties. In societies marked by high inequality, wealth signals not only status but survival: to lack it is to risk invisibility and exclusion. In wealthier nations, where basic needs are more widely met, money serves more as a marker of aspiration and self-expression, but the pressure remains relentless. Across contexts, money functions as a mirror of value, shaping not just how others see us but how we see ourselves.

The consequences are both personal and societal. Individuals who equate money with worth often struggle with chronic dissatisfaction, for there is always someone richer, more successful, or more visibly affluent. The comparison never ends. This dynamic also erodes resilience: when esteem depends on external financial markers, setbacks that are inevitable in any economic life become intolerable threats to self-identity. At the societal level, the conflation of money with worth drives unhealthy levels of debt, overwork, and exploitation, as people chase validation at the expense of well-being. *The pursuit of wealth, framed as a pursuit of self-worth, is never satisfied, because identity cannot be secured by numbers alone.*

There are, however, counterpoints worth considering. Some argue that linking money and worth is not entirely negative. Financial success can indeed reflect discipline, creativity, or resilience, and recognition of achievement can bolster confidence and fuel further growth. To sever all connection between money and esteem would be naïve. The danger lies in over-identification, where worth becomes wholly contingent on financial standing. A balanced view recognises money as one aspect of life performance but not its total measure. *Self-worth must be anchored in qualities that money cannot capture—integrity, relationships, creativity, contribution—if it is to withstand the inevitable fluctuations of fortune.*

Breaking the identification between money and worth requires both cognitive and cultural shifts. On the personal level, practices such as journaling or therapy can help individuals trace the origins of their financial identity and disentangle it from self-esteem. Reflecting on formative messages—parental attitudes toward money, societal expectations, personal experiences of success or failure—can illuminate why money feels so tied to worth. On the cultural level, promoting alternative narratives of value is essential. Highlighting achievements in service, art, or intellectual contribution can expand the horizons of what is considered worthy.

Examples of resistance already exist. Movements centred on minimalism, sustainability, or slow living challenge the assumption that worth equals wealth, reframing status in terms of simplicity, ecological responsibility, or community. Philanthropy and social entrepreneurship offer another model, where financial success is measured not only by accumulation but by impact. These shifts demonstrate that identity need not be tethered to financial metrics alone. Yet they also underscore how difficult it is to loosen the grip of money on self-worth: even countercultural movements often generate their own markets, with new forms of status consumption replacing old ones.

Ultimately, the link between money and self-worth is less a flaw of individual psychology than a reflection of broader cultural logic. When economies reward productivity, societies lionise wealth, and media celebrate affluence, individuals inevitably absorb the lesson that to be more is to have more. The challenge is not simply to reject this logic but to critically examine and reframe it. *True self-worth is not found in the balance sheet but in the capacity to live meaningfully, relate authentically, and contribute beyond the self.* Money may enhance or diminish these pursuits, but it cannot define them. Recognising this is not an escape from financial responsibility but a liberation from its tyranny—a reminder that value lies not in what one owns, but in who one is.

The "Rich" and "Poor" Identities

One of the most powerful forces shaping financial behaviour is not an external constraint but an internalised identity. Long before numbers are added up on a bank statement, people adopt labels about who they are financially—labels that act like silent scripts guiding their expectations, decisions, and sense of possibility. To be "rich" or "poor" is not merely to hold a certain amount of money; it is to inhabit a psychological and cultural category that influences how one thinks, feels, and acts around money. These identities, once accepted, become self-fulfilling. *The danger is not only in being materially limited but in being mentally confined by the labels society and individuals apply to themselves.*

From early childhood, cues about money identity are absorbed long before one learns to budget or invest. A child growing up in a family where bills are always overdue may unconsciously internalise the message: "people like us never get ahead." Even if they later earn a stable income, this early script can undermine confidence, leading them to underestimate what is possible. Conversely, a child raised in affluence may adopt the identity of being "naturally comfortable," and this expectation can persist even when reality shifts, driving them into debt in an attempt to maintain an inherited self-image. The label does not merely describe circumstances; it prescribes behaviour.

What makes these identities particularly resilient is their ability to offer psychological safety. The "poor" identity, though limiting, can become a shield against disappointment. If one already expects financial struggle, failure comes as confirmation rather than shock. On the other hand, those who see themselves as "rich" often resist acknowledging setbacks because it threatens not just their balance sheet but their sense of self. They may double down on risky ventures or overspending to protect the image they have cultivated. *In both cases, identity operates as a filter, distorting reality to fit a pre-existing narrative.*

Research in behavioural economics supports this view. Studies on "scarcity mindset" show that individuals who identify as poor, regardless of actual income level, tend to exhibit reduced cognitive bandwidth, tunnelled focus on short-term survival, and difficulty planning for the future. Importantly, these patterns are not simply the result of having fewer resources but of perceiving oneself as perpetually constrained. Identity magnifies circumstance into destiny. Meanwhile, those with a "rich" identity can fall prey to overconfidence bias, assuming that opportunities will always be available and risks will always pay off. The financial crash of 2008 offered countless examples of individuals and institutions who operated under the illusion of invulnerability, rooted not only in numbers but in the identity of being part of the prosperous class.

The stickiness of these labels is reinforced by social structures. Class, race, profession, and geography often shape the expectations people set for themselves. In some communities, wealth is viewed as unattainable for "people like us," while in others, the pressure to display affluence is inescapable, regardless of actual financial stability. These narratives are perpetuated through language as well: phrases like "we're working-class," "she's old money," or "he comes from nothing" are more than descriptors—they are identity markers that imply behavioural codes. To step outside of them is to risk social friction, even ridicule.

Consider the case of first-generation university graduates who enter professional careers. Despite improved earnings, many carry the "poor" identity from their upbringing, manifesting in reluctance to invest, discomfort discussing money, or guilt when spending on themselves. Their peers, raised in more affluent households, may approach identical salaries with confidence, seeing them as natural stepping stones to greater wealth. Objectively, the incomes are equal; subjectively, the possibilities diverge dramatically. This illustrates the profound truth: *financial identity can matter as much as, if not more than, financial reality.*

There is also a paradox here worth noting. For some, embracing the "poor" identity becomes a source of resilience, fuelling determination to break free and prove society wrong. Similarly, the "rich" identity, when combined with responsibility, can instil the confidence needed to take productive risks and pursue ambitious opportunities. The issue is not that identities exist—they are inevitable—but that they become rigid, unquestioned, and totalising. Problems arise when individuals cease to see themselves as capable of inhabiting a different story.

The way out requires deliberate interrogation of these labels. Psychologists studying identity change emphasise the importance of narrative reframing: rather than adopting "I am poor" as an essential trait, one might articulate, "I am currently in a financial rebuilding phase." Similarly, replacing "I'm rich, therefore invulnerable" with "I have resources, but I must use them wisely" opens the possibility of growth and humility. *The task is not to deny reality but to resist imprisoning the self within it.*

Cultural examples underscore this principle. Many entrepreneurs who later became wealthy began with modest means but refused to internalise the "poor" identity as permanent. They acknowledged scarcity without letting it define them. Equally, individuals who have lost fortunes but rebuilt their lives often do so by detaching their sense of worth from the "rich" label, allowing themselves to adapt rather than collapse under the weight of identity loss. History is filled with stories of reinvention that demonstrate the malleability of money identities, provided individuals remain conscious of them.

The challenge is that identity feels invisible. Unlike a budget, it is not written down; unlike a salary, it is not printed on a pay slip. It resides in language, assumptions, and unconscious self-talk. One way to expose it is to notice recurring phrases: "I'll never be able to afford that," "people like me don't invest," or "I'll always have money." Such statements reveal the hidden operating system beneath behaviour. Once made visible, they can be questioned, and questioning is the first step toward transformation.

Ultimately, the labels of "rich" and "poor" are less about numbers than about narratives. To internalise them uncritically is to live within someone else's script, limiting what is seen as possible. By recognising these identities for what they are—constructs shaped by culture, family, and psychology—individuals can begin to rewrite them. The financial landscape may not change overnight, but the sense of agency does. *And once identity shifts, behaviour follows, opening the door to futures that were previously unimaginable.*

Choosing a New Identity

Few aspects of money are as underestimated as the role identity plays in shaping financial lives. People often assume that what matters most is knowledge—learning to budget, invest, or control spending. Yet beneath those practical skills lies something more fundamental: the way individuals see themselves in relation to money. If identity is shaped by comparison, by the labels of "rich" or "poor," or by inherited scripts about what people like us can or cannot do, then every decision is filtered through a narrative that may have little to do with present reality. The task of choosing a new money identity, one grounded in autonomy and values rather than external approval, is both liberating and profoundly difficult. It requires moving beyond the stories society offers and daring to write one's own.

The challenge begins with recognising that identity is rarely self-chosen. It is absorbed—through family expectations, cultural norms, professional environments, and subtle social cues. A lawyer who feels compelled to maintain a luxury lifestyle may not be acting out of conscious desire but from the script that professionalism equates to affluence. A teacher who believes that modesty is virtuous may shy away from wealth-building strategies, even if financially beneficial, because they conflict with a moral identity. In both cases, behaviour reflects a borrowed identity, not an autonomous one. *To choose a new identity, one must first confront the extent to which the current one is inherited rather than designed.*

What makes this confrontation difficult is the emotional security that comes with fitting into familiar categories. To identify as middle class, working class, or elite provides a framework of belonging. Stepping outside those frameworks can feel destabilising, even when they are limiting. Sociologists have long observed how people police themselves to remain consistent with the groups they identify with. Overspending to keep pace with friends, or under-earning because ambition feels like betrayal of one's roots, are not isolated quirks—they are expressions of identity loyalty. This loyalty, though invisible, can be stronger than rational calculation. If financial identities are fundamentally social, then redefining them requires courage to withstand social friction.

The path toward a new identity is not about rejecting belonging but about shifting the axis on which belonging rests. Instead of being defined by external comparisons—am I richer than my peers, poorer than my neighbour, as successful as my parents expected?—identity can be anchored in personal values. A person who values autonomy may shape a money identity that prioritises flexibility over status, choosing freelance work and modest living over corporate prestige. Another who values contribution may orient spending and saving around supporting causes and communities, regardless of whether it appears financially "impressive" to others. In both cases, the key is that identity is tied to values chosen consciously, not expectations imposed externally.

Psychological research offers tools for this process. Identity-based behaviour change, a growing field of study, shows that people are more likely to sustain habits when those habits reinforce who they believe themselves to be. For example, saying "I am the kind of person who manages money wisely" is more powerful than saying "I want to save more." The first creates a shift in self-concept, the second merely sets a temporary goal. *Redefining reward in terms of identity alignment—seeing each decision as a reinforcement of one's chosen values—transforms financial discipline from deprivation into self-expression.*

Yet there is tension to address. Choosing a new identity does not mean creating a fantasy detached from reality. It is not helpful to declare "I am wealthy" while ignoring debt. Nor does it mean discarding every cultural or familial influence; heritage and community can provide grounding values. The point is not to erase identity but to reclaim authorship. Consider the difference between someone who avoids investing because "people like me don't do that" and someone who chooses not to invest in speculative assets because "my values are stability and stewardship." The behaviour might appear similar—avoiding risk—but one emerges from constraint, the other from autonomy. *It is not the act itself but the origin of the choice that defines whether it expresses freedom or fear.*

Examples from everyday life illuminate this distinction. A professional who rejects the endless cycle of status-driven upgrades—new car, bigger home, luxury holidays—may feel pressure from peers but experience deep alignment in knowing their identity is not tied to performance theatre. Similarly, someone from a modest background who embraces investing and entrepreneurship is not betraying their roots but choosing to expand what those roots make possible. In both cases, the individual steps outside of comparison and into coherence with values, demonstrating that new identities are less about what money buys and more about what money represents.

One practical method for fostering such change is to make values explicit. When values remain vague, comparison fills the vacuum. If one has not articulated whether they prize autonomy, security, creativity, or generosity, then financial choices will default to mimicking others. But when values are written down, revisited, and linked to specific money decisions, they become a compass. Every purchase or investment can be measured not against peers but against self-chosen standards. This does not eliminate difficulty—societal comparison is deeply ingrained—but it provides an anchor strong enough to resist it.

Philosophically, this reframing challenges the idea that worth is externally bestowed. For centuries, societies have equated wealth with virtue, associating prosperity with industriousness or divine favour, and poverty with failure. Breaking free from that narrative requires recognising that money is a tool, not an essence. A new identity rooted in values refuses to use net worth as shorthand for self-worth. Instead, it asks: what kind of person am I becoming through the way I earn, spend, save, and give? The answers are not numbers but orientations—toward freedom, dignity, connection, creativity.

The long-term effect of this shift is profound. When money identity is no longer tethered to external comparison, financial behaviour changes naturally. Saving is no longer a grim act of self-denial but a reinforcement of autonomy. Spending is no longer an unconscious attempt to belong but an intentional choice aligned with joy or generosity. Even in difficult times, identity provides resilience. A setback in income does not mean a collapse in self-concept, because identity is anchored in values that endure beyond circumstance. *The individual is no longer rich or poor, successful or failed, but coherent with themselves.*

To choose a new identity around money is therefore to choose freedom—not the abstract freedom of unlimited wealth, but the practical freedom of alignment between values and behaviour. It is a demanding task, because it requires unlearning comparisons that have been rehearsed for a lifetime. Yet it is also empowering, because once chosen, the new identity becomes a foundation for every future decision. By moving away from labels imposed by others and into identities consciously claimed, individuals reclaim authorship of their financial story. And in doing so, they discover that the most valuable currency is not money itself but the autonomy to define what it means.

Chapter 9
Rewriting the Money Mind

For most people, financial change is approached as a technical exercise: learn the formulas, apply the rules, stick to the budget. Yet the evidence of lived experience tells a more complicated story. Knowledge alone does not alter behaviour. People who can recite compound interest calculations still carry credit card balances; those who understand the dangers of overspending find themselves at the till with unplanned purchases. The gap between knowing and doing is not one of intelligence but of mind. Our money habits are not neutral calculations—they are scripts, emotional reflexes, and identity markers repeated until they feel inevitable. To transform them requires more than information; it requires rewriting the money mind itself.

The premise of rewriting is that financial decisions are not isolated acts but expressions of deeper patterns. Each swipe of a card, each delayed bill payment, each avoided account statement is part of a narrative. Some of these narratives originate in childhood—lessons from parents, family dynamics around scarcity or abundance, silent messages absorbed when money was a source of stress or pride. Others are shaped by cultural context, where belonging may demand spending on appearances or where security is defined by visible assets. Still others are born from immediate emotional triggers: boredom, loneliness, envy, fatigue. The key point is that *behaviour is rarely irrational once the underlying script is made visible.* To change behaviour, one must first see the script in action. Awareness becomes the first currency of transformation.

But awareness, though essential, is easily misunderstood. Noticing a habit is not the same as criticising it. Too often, people approach money mindfulness with self-judgment: "I am terrible with money," "I have no discipline," "I will never change." Such judgments paradoxically reinforce the very patterns they aim to break, entrenching a sense of identity that binds future behaviour. The alternative is financial mindfulness, a practice of observing behaviour without condemnation. Journaling daily expenses, tracking emotional states alongside spending, or pausing briefly before a purchase to register the feeling driving it—these are acts not of policing but of inquiry. *When we shift from judging to observing, we create space between trigger and response, and in that space lies the possibility of new choices.*

Practical tools for building this space are deceptively simple. A notebook carried in a pocket, a banking app checked at the same time each evening, or a weekly reflection on how money was spent can reveal patterns that otherwise remain invisible. A person who repeatedly buys takeaway after difficult meetings is not simply "bad with money" but soothing stress through convenience. Another who postpones looking at bills until reminders arrive is not lazy but avoiding the discomfort of confrontation. Recognising these links does not excuse behaviour but contextualises it. And once contextualised, the cycle can be disrupted.

Disruption is the second phase of rewriting the money mind. Old patterns are powerful because they are automatic; the brain conserves energy by defaulting to familiar scripts, even when costly. Interrupting those scripts requires inserting friction at the point of decision. This might mean leaving credit cards at home to force reflection before a purchase, or instituting a 24-hour rule before non-essential spending. For those prone to avoidance, disruption might involve scheduling a recurring "money check-in" at a set time, treating it as non-negotiable as brushing one's teeth. Each small disruption is not merely behavioural but neurological, rewiring pathways by replacing habit loops with conscious choice.

Yet interruption alone cannot sustain change. Willpower is finite; what endures are systems that make good behaviour the path of least resistance. Designing better defaults turns effortful choices into effortless ones. Automatic transfers into savings accounts, pre-committed retirement contributions, or bill payments scheduled in advance remove the need for constant vigilance. Just as important are defaults that add friction to destructive behaviour: unsubscribing from marketing emails, removing saved payment details from websites, or setting withdrawal limits on accounts. These systems transform discipline from a daily battle into a structural advantage. *Freedom is not achieved by constant exertion but by reshaping the environment so that the better choice becomes the easier one.*

At a deeper level, rewriting the money mind is not simply about avoiding mistakes but about reshaping identity. When people interrupt destructive patterns and design supportive systems, they are not just managing money—they are telling themselves a new story about who they are. A person who once identified as "hopeless with money" can, through repeated acts of mindfulness and small victories, come to see themselves as "the kind of person who takes care of financial wellbeing." This shift in identity is not superficial; it is the anchor that sustains change when motivation fades. Behaviour aligned with identity becomes self-reinforcing.

The implications reach beyond the individual. Collectively, our money minds shape societies. When enough people adopt new scripts—valuing long-term stability over short-term consumption, prioritising autonomy over comparison—the financial culture itself shifts. Advertising loses some of its manipulative force when consumers recognise the triggers it exploits. Debt loses some of its stigma when people speak openly about avoidance and shame. Saving becomes less about deprivation and more about empowerment when reframed as alignment with chosen values. In this sense, rewriting the money mind is not only a personal act but a cultural intervention.

The chapters that follow will equip readers with specific practices for each of these stages: cultivating awareness as the foundation, building non-judgmental financial mindfulness, interrupting destructive loops with practical tools, and designing better defaults that automate supportive habits. But the introduction here serves to highlight the stakes. Without rewriting the money mind, technical knowledge will always be undermined by hidden scripts. With it, even modest incomes can support autonomy, dignity, and fulfilment. *The true measure of financial success is not how much money is accumulated but how consciously and freely it is used.*

Rewriting, then, is less about perfecting spreadsheets and more about reclaiming authorship. It is the shift from being acted upon by unconscious habits to actively shaping them; from living in inherited narratives to constructing deliberate ones; from financial anxiety as background noise to financial clarity as lived practice. This chapter opens not with the promise of easy fixes but with the recognition of power—the power to see, to interrupt, and to design. For those willing to engage with that power, the act of rewriting is not a burden but a profound opportunity: the chance to create a money mind that reflects not the demands of the past but the possibilities of the future.

Awareness as First Currency

Change does not begin with action; it begins with awareness. Before new habits can take root or old ones can be replaced, there must be recognition—of the scripts that guide behaviour, the emotions that drive decisions, and the triggers that set them in motion. In the world of money, this recognition is not a luxury but a prerequisite. Without it, even the most carefully designed budgets or investment strategies collapse under the weight of unexamined impulses. Awareness functions as the first currency of financial transformation: the resource that makes every subsequent choice possible.

Consider a person who finds themselves repeatedly overspending on clothes. On the surface, it looks like a failure of discipline or an indulgence in vanity. But if observed closely, the purchase is less about fabric and fashion and more about the feeling it promises. Perhaps it provides temporary relief from stress, or validation after a difficult week at work, or even the fleeting thrill of novelty. To address the behaviour without recognising these drivers is to misdiagnose the problem. This is why financial advice, when it ignores psychology, so often fails: *you cannot change what you cannot see.* Awareness does not eliminate the desire to buy, but it reframes it, allowing a person to ask, "What am I really purchasing here—the item, or the feeling?"

The difficulty lies in the fact that scripts often operate below consciousness. Many people can recall growing up with statements like "money doesn't grow on trees" or "we can't afford that," phrases repeated so often they became invisible truths. Others inherit subtle cultural messages about what is respectable or irresponsible spending. These scripts do not announce themselves; they simply shape choices until they feel like common sense. Awareness requires surfacing these narratives, not in order to assign blame, but to bring them into the light where they can be questioned. *The act of naming a script is the first step towards loosening its hold.*

Emotions play an equally powerful role. Neuroscience has shown that decision-making is not a cold, rational process but deeply interwoven with feeling. Anxiety, pride, shame, envy, and excitement can all distort financial choices. Someone in a state of stress may reach for the quick fix of retail therapy, not because it makes logical sense but because it soothes in the moment. Conversely, another person paralysed by fear of scarcity may hoard money compulsively, even at the cost of joy and opportunity. In both cases, the individual believes they are "managing money," when in reality money is managing them. Awareness invites a pause long enough to notice the emotion at play. By asking, "Am I making this decision from fear, pride, or calm deliberation?" one introduces a crucial layer of reflection that transforms the nature of the choice.

Triggers are the final piece in this triad. They are the cues that set scripts and emotions into motion. For some, the trigger is environmental: walking past a sale sign, scrolling through social media, or entering a familiar café. For others, it is internal: the boredom of a quiet evening, the fatigue after work, or the sense of deserving a treat after an achievement. Triggers are not inherently negative, but when left unacknowledged, they hijack behaviour. Awareness transforms a trigger from a silent command into an observable event. A person who recognises that they crave online shopping late at night is better equipped to disrupt the cycle than one who sees only the aftermath of another delivery box on the doorstep.

One of the most striking features of awareness is its capacity to shift responsibility from self-condemnation to self-understanding. The dominant financial culture often frames missteps in moral terms—"reckless spending," "irresponsible debt," "bad with money." Such labels reduce complex patterns to character flaws, leaving individuals trapped in shame. Yet shame rarely produces lasting change; it usually fuels further avoidance or self-sabotage. Awareness, by contrast, reframes the struggle. Instead of "I am reckless," the insight becomes, "I spend more when I am lonely." Instead of "I am bad with money," it becomes, "I have inherited a scarcity script that makes me anxious about spending." These reframings do not absolve accountability, but they make it constructive rather than paralysing.

Modern behavioural research supports this reorientation. Studies in behavioural economics show that people are highly susceptible to cognitive biases—loss aversion, present bias, anchoring—that operate beneath conscious thought. Simply becoming aware of these biases can reduce their influence. For instance, recognising that the brain perceives saving as a loss rather than a gain helps explain why people resist putting money aside. With awareness, one can reframe the act of saving not as deprivation but as future security, a reframing that changes the emotional experience of the behaviour. Again, the principle holds: *what is noticed can be reframed, and what is reframed can be changed.*

Awareness also creates the foundation for accountability. A journal of expenses, paired with reflections on the circumstances around each purchase, is more than a record of transactions; it is a map of the inner landscape of money. Patterns emerge: spikes in spending after stressful meetings, reluctance to invest in personal development despite other discretionary spending, or a tendency to give generously to friends while neglecting one's own needs. Each entry becomes data for reflection. Over time, this kind of awareness creates a richer picture than any bank statement could provide, because it connects numbers with narratives.

Yet awareness alone is not enough—it is a beginning, not a destination. There is a risk of mistaking observation for transformation, of believing that seeing a pattern automatically changes it. In practice, awareness is more like the turning of a key in a lock. The door may open, but one must still step through. Still, without the key, the door remains closed. Many people attempt to "fix" their money problems without this key, jumping straight into action—restrictive budgets, rigid saving plans, aggressive debt repayment strategies—only to relapse when old triggers resurface. Awareness ensures that change is built on understanding rather than suppression.

The practical implication is that cultivating awareness should be treated as a deliberate practice, not an incidental by-product. Journaling, mindful reflection, regular check-ins, or even working with a therapist or coach are not auxiliary tasks; they are central to building financial stability. These practices create the space to recognise scripts, identify emotional drivers, and anticipate triggers before they dictate behaviour. In a sense, they create a "pause button" in a world that constantly pushes toward instant action. *That pause, however brief, is where freedom begins.*

Perhaps the most powerful feature of awareness is its cumulative nature. The first insights may be modest: noticing that one shops more on Fridays, or that bills are consistently delayed out of dread. But over time, these small observations compound, much like financial interest. They deepen into a sophisticated self-understanding: recognising that overspending is tied to an unmet need for validation, or that avoidance stems from fear of reliving childhood financial insecurity. With each layer uncovered, the ability to act with clarity and intention grows. Awareness, then, is not a static event but an evolving process, one that continually equips individuals to respond to new challenges with resilience.

In the end, awareness does more than expose the mechanics of behaviour—it reshapes identity. To notice is to step outside the automatic pilot of old patterns and to assert authorship over one's financial life. It is to move from being a passive subject of scripts, emotions, and triggers to being an observer capable of choice. And once choice enters the picture, new narratives become possible. Awareness is not only the first currency of change; it is the currency that gives value to every other effort, ensuring that financial decisions are not driven by ghosts of the past or impulses of the present, but by deliberate alignment with who one wishes to become.

Building Financial Mindfulness

Most people think of money management as a technical skill—something solved by budgeting software, investment strategies, or financial advice columns. Yet, in practice, the decisive factor is not information but awareness. The challenge is not that people do not know they should spend less than they earn, but that their behaviour is shaped by habits and emotions that operate beneath conscious thought. Here lies the value of financial mindfulness: the practice of observing money behaviour without judgement. By noticing patterns with clarity rather than criticism, individuals create the space to make different choices, breaking cycles that no spreadsheet can resolve on its own.

Mindfulness, in its original sense, is not about eliminating thought or emotion but recognising them as they arise. Applied to money, this means shifting attention from the mechanical recording of transactions to the subtler awareness of what each transaction represents. A coffee purchased on the way to work, for example, is not only a financial act but also a reflection of routine, comfort, or identity. The question is not whether the purchase is good or bad, but what need it serves, what feeling it satisfies, and whether it aligns with larger goals. *When money behaviour is observed without the harsh lens of judgement, it becomes a source of insight rather than shame.*

Consider the act of journaling. A financial journal is not merely an account of pounds spent; it is a mirror of the internal landscape. Writing down what was bought, why it was bought, and how one felt before and after creates a record that is both objective and deeply personal. Over time, patterns emerge: the stress-driven purchases that follow difficult meetings, the avoidance of checking accounts after indulgent weekends, the reluctance to invest in oneself while freely spending on others. Such awareness transforms financial data into human data. Importantly, journaling creates a narrative continuity that numbers alone cannot provide, allowing individuals to see their financial lives as stories rather than isolated incidents.

Tracking, by contrast, introduces structure. Where journaling engages reflection, tracking builds consistency. Mobile apps and bank dashboards now make it easier than ever to see spending in categories: groceries, transport, entertainment. But technology alone does not create mindfulness; it must be coupled with interpretation. A tracked expense is only a statistic until one asks what it means. Does the pattern reflect values, or does it reflect impulse? Does it show an investment in health and relationships, or does it reveal automaticity and neglect? Tracking done without judgement prevents defensive reactions—"I'm bad with money"—and replaces them with curiosity—"What does this tell me about myself?"

Reflection ties the two practices together. To reflect is to step back, not with self-reproach but with inquiry. It asks, "What am I learning about myself through my financial behaviour?" Reflection can take the form of a weekly review, a conversation with a trusted partner, or a moment of pause before large expenditures. The power of reflection lies in its capacity to break the binary of success and failure. A person who overspends is not "failing," but engaging in behaviour that can be examined, understood, and adjusted. *Reflection replaces guilt with learning, and learning fuels change.*

The difficulty is that financial culture is saturated with judgement. Advertisements imply what a "successful" lifestyle should look like, while financial advice often carries a moralising tone: spend less, save more, avoid mistakes. In such an environment, people are quick to defend, rationalise, or hide their choices. Mindfulness disrupts this cycle by removing the moral weight. Observing that one spends excessively when lonely does not condemn the spender as weak; it simply reveals the role of loneliness in shaping financial decisions. This awareness opens possibilities: addressing loneliness directly rather than numbing it with purchases.

Neuroscience supports this approach. Studies show that mindfulness alters the brain's response to craving and stress by activating regions associated with self-regulation and reducing the automaticity of impulsive behaviour. Translated into financial terms, mindfulness creates a gap between the trigger and the response. Instead of moving from desire straight to purchase, the mindful individual pauses long enough to ask whether the purchase serves a genuine need. This pause does not eliminate desire but changes its power. *Mindfulness shifts behaviour from compulsion to choice.*

There is also a broader philosophical dimension. Financial mindfulness challenges the prevailing narrative that wealth is purely external—measured in bank balances, assets, and possessions. Instead, it treats money as relational: a reflection of inner states, values, and identities. The mindful person recognises that each pound spent is a statement of what is prioritised, consciously or unconsciously. To be mindful is to ensure that these statements align with one's chosen identity rather than inherited scripts or social pressures. It is, in essence, to treat money not as an end in itself but as a medium through which a meaningful life is crafted.

Case studies illustrate the difference. A young professional who regularly eats out may discover, through journaling, that the behaviour is less about convenience and more about avoiding the loneliness of eating alone. With this insight, the "problem" of overspending is no longer simply financial; it becomes an invitation to address the underlying need for connection. Another individual may find that their compulsive saving stems not from prudence but from fear, rooted in childhood scarcity. Awareness allows them to recognise that accumulating money while depriving themselves of joy is not security but avoidance. In both cases, mindfulness transforms the narrative from self-blame to self-discovery.

Sceptics might argue that mindfulness risks becoming a form of indulgent navel-gazing, a way of endlessly reflecting without taking action. But the purpose is not reflection for its own sake; it is to ensure that action is informed rather than reactive. Just as athletes review footage of their performance to improve, financial mindfulness provides the feedback loop that makes deliberate improvement possible. Without it, change is reduced to willpower alone, a resource notoriously unreliable under stress. With it, change becomes systemic, supported by insight and self-compassion.

The long-term benefit of financial mindfulness is resilience. Economic uncertainty, job transitions, family obligations—all can destabilise even the most carefully planned finances. But a person grounded in awareness is less likely to be thrown off course. They recognise their emotional responses, anticipate their triggers, and return more quickly to balance after disruption. They are not perfect, but they are adaptable. *Mindfulness does not guarantee wealth, but it cultivates stability of mind—the foundation on which wealth, in every sense of the word, can grow.*

In practice, building financial mindfulness is less about adopting a single technique than about cultivating an ongoing stance of observation. Whether through journaling, digital tracking, or

reflective pauses, the aim is the same: to replace unconscious automaticity with conscious awareness. Each small act of noticing becomes a seed of freedom, gradually replacing cycles of shame and avoidance with cycles of clarity and choice. Over time, the result is not only better financial outcomes but a more coherent relationship with money itself—one marked not by fear or compulsion but by alignment with values and deliberate living.

Interrupting the Old Patterns

Automaticity is both the brain's strength and its greatest liability. We survive by turning repeated behaviours into habits, freeing up mental energy for other tasks. Yet the very mechanism that allows us to brush our teeth without thinking also ensures that financial missteps—impulse spending, avoidance of bills, compulsive scrolling through online shops—become self-reinforcing routines. The challenge is that once a pattern is encoded in the brain's circuitry, it rarely dissolves on its own. *Interruption, deliberate and repeated, is the only way to reclaim choice from autopilot.*

The problem is not ignorance. Few people overspend because they are unaware of the concept of budgeting. The real barrier is that in the heat of a trigger—stress, fatigue, boredom—the brain defaults to its established response. The swipe of a card or the click of a checkout button delivers instant relief, and the cost is postponed. Avoidance works in much the same way: unopened bank statements protect self-image in the short term but deepen anxiety in the long run. To interrupt these loops requires not just willpower but strategies designed to destabilise the automatic chain between trigger and behaviour.

One of the most effective tools is the introduction of friction. Automatic spending thrives on ease; disruption thrives on inconvenience. For example, deleting stored payment information from online retailers introduces a moment's pause. Setting up bank accounts that require two-step verification for transfers forces reflection. Even the simple act of leaving a credit card at home ensures that purchasing decisions require intention rather than impulse. The aim is not to remove temptation altogether, which is often impossible, but to insert enough delay that awareness can catch up with desire. *Friction converts unconscious behaviour into conscious choice.*

Another intervention is substitution. The brain rarely responds well to sheer suppression; telling oneself "don't spend" without an alternative usually intensifies the urge. Instead, replacing the behaviour with a different but equally soothing action proves more sustainable. A person accustomed to buying takeaway coffee during stressful afternoons might substitute the ritual with a short walk or a call to a friend. Both meet the underlying need for comfort or a break but avoid the automatic expense. Over time, the brain rewires not by eliminating reward but by associating reward with healthier cues.

Visual interruption can also be powerful. Research in behavioural economics shows that people often act as though money were abstract when it is represented by numbers on a screen. Making finances visible in more tangible ways reactivates emotional engagement. For instance, printing out monthly statements and placing them where they cannot be ignored, or tracking spending with coloured charts that highlight cumulative effects, interrupts the mind's tendency to rationalise small purchases. The cumulative becomes concrete, and patterns that once slipped under awareness become undeniable.

Interruption, however, is not only about disrupting overspending. It is equally necessary for avoidance. The human tendency to delay unpleasant tasks—opening bills, reviewing debt balances—is itself a habit loop: anxiety creates avoidance, avoidance creates more anxiety, and the cycle tightens. To break it, some employ the "two-minute rule": committing to engage with the avoided task for only two minutes. Often the barrier is not the task itself but the emotional weight attached to it. By lowering the threshold of engagement, the avoidance pattern is interrupted, and once started, the task frequently continues beyond the initial two minutes. This reframes financial responsibility not as an overwhelming ordeal but as a series of manageable micro-steps.

There is also value in social interruption. Many financial behaviours thrive in secrecy, protected from scrutiny by silence. Sharing goals

Chapter 10
Habits of Wealth Beyond Income

Wealth, as most societies define it, is a number. It is an account balance, a net worth calculation, a target set by financial advisors or whispered in comparison among peers. Yet beneath these numerical measures lies a deeper, more elusive truth: money alone does not determine whether people feel wealthy. Some who command vast fortunes remain anxious, restless, and insatiable, while others with modest means radiate a sense of sufficiency that cannot be captured by income statements. This paradox forces us to re-examine the foundations of financial well-being. If wealth were simply a matter of earning more, then all high earners would live free from insecurity. The evidence, however, reveals the opposite. In surveys across income brackets, financial stress does not vanish at higher levels of earnings; it often intensifies. The difference lies not in the zeros added to a salary but in the habits of mind and practice that shape how people relate to money. This chapter turns to those habits—the psychological, emotional, and behavioural patterns that allow wealth to exist beyond income itself.

The first of these is the recognition of *enough*. The cultural script of modern capitalism insists that "more" is always better: more possessions, more upgrades, more security, more prestige. Yet this endless pursuit is structurally unresolvable, because the benchmarks shift as soon as they are reached. To chase wealth defined only by accumulation is to live in permanent dissatisfaction. By contrast, those who cultivate a sense of sufficiency recognise that wealth is not merely the ability to acquire but the ability to choose. *Enough is not scarcity dressed as contentment; it is the active acknowledgement that one has reached a point where choice, not compulsion, governs decisions.* This perspective frees individuals from the treadmill of comparison, making space for a different kind of financial confidence—one rooted not in what is still lacking, but in what is already secured.

The transformation from fear to agency further deepens this redefinition. Many people navigate money with an undercurrent of anxiety: the dread of unexpected bills, the guilt of past decisions, the shame of not "measuring up" to some external standard. Fear constrains action. It narrows perspective, leading individuals to either over-control every financial detail or avoid engaging with their finances altogether. Reframing money as a medium of agency shifts the emphasis. Decisions are no longer desperate attempts to avoid catastrophe but expressions of values and priorities. Choosing to save becomes not a denial of pleasure but an assertion of independence. Choosing to spend thoughtfully becomes not indulgence but a reflection of identity. *When money is treated as a tool of agency rather than a measure of deficiency, anxiety loses its hold.*

Gratitude and contentment play an essential role in this process. Psychological research shows that gratitude reduces the tendency to overconsume by shifting attention away from what is absent and toward what is present. In financial terms, gratitude is not passive acceptance but an active reorientation of perception. A person who regularly acknowledges the adequacy of their current circumstances is less vulnerable to the pull of envy or status competition. Contentment, too, is often misunderstood. It is not complacency or a refusal to strive; it is the ability to pursue goals without tying identity to their attainment. In a consumer-driven culture, cultivating these states of mind is profoundly countercultural. Yet they reduce destructive money behaviours—impulse spending, reckless borrowing, compulsive upgrading—by loosening the grip of imagined deficiency. The wealthiest people are not always those with the greatest assets, but often those who can look at their lives and perceive richness in what already exists.

Finally, wealth must be seen as a practice rather than a fixed destination. Traditional narratives imply that financial success is a point one eventually arrives at: a salary level, a savings milestone, a retirement figure. But this view overlooks the fluid, ongoing nature of financial life. Circumstances change, markets fluctuate, health shifts, relationships evolve. To treat wealth as a destination is to anchor identity in a fragile and shifting ground. A more sustainable approach is to view financial well-being as a practice—an ongoing set of habits and mindsets maintained with mindfulness. Just as physical health is not achieved once and for all by reaching a target weight but by daily attention to movement, nutrition, and rest, so financial health is sustained through continuous, deliberate practice. Automating savings, reflecting on spending, adjusting goals, and cultivating gratitude are not one-time achievements but recurring exercises. *Wealth, in this sense, is not a product of arrival but of repetition.*

This chapter, then, reframes the very definition of financial success. It challenges the reader to look beyond the seductive but ultimately hollow markers of income and net worth. It invites a more profound exploration of sufficiency, agency, gratitude, and practice—elements that, once cultivated, generate a form of wealth no market fluctuation can erode. The reader will come to see that the true habits of wealth are not restricted to those with extraordinary incomes. They are accessible, practicable, and transformative for anyone willing to engage. By the end of this exploration, wealth will no longer appear as a finish line in the distance but as a set of lived practices embedded in daily choices. This redefinition is not only intellectually rigorous but also deeply liberating: it places the experience of wealth within reach not as a matter of luck or inheritance, but as the product of cultivated habits that transcend income altogether.

The Psychology of Enough – Challenges the endless pursuit of "more" and redefines wealth as sufficiency plus choice

Few ideas are more deeply ingrained in modern culture than the assumption that happiness expands in direct proportion to income. The conviction that more is always better drives careers, consumer habits, and even entire economic systems. Yet behind this relentless pursuit lies a paradox: despite rising global wealth, surveys consistently reveal stagnant or declining levels of life satisfaction in many affluent societies. The gap between having more and feeling well is not accidental; it is structural. Human beings are wired to adapt to improvements and recalibrate expectations. What once felt like prosperity quickly becomes normal, and normal soon feels insufficient. The pursuit of "more" is not an endpoint but a treadmill—what psychologists term the *hedonic adaptation.* Unless consciously examined, this treadmill ensures that enough is never truly reached, no matter how high the income or how plentiful the possessions.

The psychology of enough begins by recognising the distinction between sufficiency and excess. Sufficiency is not deprivation masked as virtue; it is the state where one's needs are met and one retains the agency to choose. It does not eliminate desire but reframes it. Excess, by contrast, is the accumulation beyond utility, often pursued to signal status or assuage insecurity rather than to enhance lived experience. Consider the household that upgrades its kitchen every five years not because the old one no longer functions but because new designs have shifted the standard of acceptability. This cycle, repeated across cars, clothing, holidays, and technology, locks individuals into a financial pattern where resources flow towards ever-receding benchmarks. *Enough interrupts this cycle by asking: what level of material provision secures dignity, flexibility, and freedom—and when does more simply become noise?*

The idea of sufficiency is deeply countercultural, yet history offers examples of its power. Ancient philosophies such as Stoicism and Buddhism emphasised moderation not merely as moral restraint but as a path to clarity. The Stoics advised that freedom resided not in multiplying possessions but in limiting dependency on them. In modern terms, sufficiency allows individuals to redirect attention from endless acquisition to meaningful agency. This does not mean rejecting ambition or innovation. Rather, it means distinguishing between growth that genuinely expands possibility and growth that simply layers complexity onto life. A professional might pursue a promotion not only for higher pay but for increased influence, autonomy, or intellectual challenge. But when the pay rise is consumed by an upgraded home, car, and lifestyle that lock the person into longer working hours and heightened stress, the illusion of progress masks a decline in freedom. *Enough is reached when accumulation ceases to serve choice and begins to erode it.*

The endless pursuit of more is reinforced by social comparison. People rarely evaluate their own wealth in absolute terms; instead, they measure themselves against peers. Research demonstrates that individuals earning a high salary may still feel poor if surrounded by those earning more, while those with modest means can feel affluent if their community shares similar standards. This relativity makes the psychology of enough difficult to sustain, because "enough" shifts with one's reference group. Yet it also reveals the central fallacy:

wealth defined only in comparative terms is inherently unstable. To base sufficiency on autonomy rather than status is to liberate oneself from the tyranny of shifting social benchmarks. The person who decides, for instance, that working four days a week provides sufficient income while preserving time for family or creative pursuits has chosen sufficiency over escalation. Their sense of wealth lies not in matching a neighbour's lifestyle but in aligning resources with values.

Real-world examples illustrate how sufficiency plus choice creates resilience. Consider households that embrace financial independence movements, not in the extreme forms that demand spartan living, but in pragmatic ways that prioritise agency. A teacher who consciously resists the cycle of upgrading possessions may not out-earn a corporate lawyer, but she may achieve a form of wealth the lawyer struggles to access: the ability to work fewer hours, retire earlier, or devote energy to passions outside the office. Here, sufficiency is not scarcity; it is the recognition that *enough* allows for choice, and choice is the true currency of wealth. By contrast, individuals who continually escalate their lifestyle in proportion to income often remain trapped in what has been called the "earn–spend–borrow" cycle, where increased pay yields little additional freedom because expectations have risen in tandem.

Critics might argue that the pursuit of more fuels innovation and economic growth. Indeed, much of the progress in living standards has stemmed from the human desire to improve. The question, however, is not whether growth is valuable but whether equating personal worth with endless acquisition is sustainable. The pursuit of more at the societal level may drive invention, but at the individual level it often drives anxiety. The tension between aspiration and sufficiency requires balance: one can pursue excellence without assuming that every gain must translate into material escalation. The psychology of enough does not advocate complacency; it advocates discernment. *It asks whether a pursuit expands autonomy or simply feeds comparison.*

One of the most striking aspects of sufficiency is its relationship to security. Many assume that only abundant wealth can provide safety from uncertainty. Yet evidence suggests that beyond a threshold where basic needs and moderate comforts are met, additional accumulation contributes little to perceived security. Anxiety about losing wealth often increases with higher assets, as more is at stake. By contrast, those who define wealth as sufficiency plus choice can experience security through adaptability: the knowledge that their well-being is not wholly tethered to fluctuating income or possessions. In practice, this might mean maintaining a lifestyle deliberately below one's maximum means, thus ensuring that setbacks do not destroy financial or emotional stability. Security, then, becomes less about fortifying walls of excess and more about cultivating resilience through sufficiency.

Philosophically, the psychology of enough reframes the question of wealth from "How much do I have?" to "How much freedom does what I have provide?" It shifts the measure from accumulation to agency, from comparison to contentment. Wealth is no longer judged by its ability to impress but by its ability to align life with values. This redefinition opens space for a healthier relationship with money—one that honours ambition without succumbing to its distortions. It invites a reflective pause in a culture of perpetual acceleration. To ask what is enough is not to lower standards but to elevate discernment.

By challenging the endless pursuit of more, the psychology of enough illuminates a path toward a more stable, humane, and meaningful conception of wealth. It demonstrates that sufficiency, when coupled with choice, can liberate individuals from cycles of dissatisfaction and anchor them in a sense of autonomy that no external comparison can erode. Far from being a retreat from ambition, this mindset provides the foundation for enduring financial well-being. It is the antidote to the treadmill of "more," offering not only clarity but the rarest form of wealth: peace with what one already holds, and the freedom to decide what truly matters next.

From Fear to Agency – Shows how reframing money decisions as expressions of control and values reduces anxiety

Fear is one of the most consistent emotional companions of money. It emerges in the dread of opening bank statements, in the unease of taking financial risks, and in the silent anxiety that lingers even when accounts are technically secure. Money fear is not simply about arithmetic; it is about identity, security, and control. For many people, financial decisions feel like a series of potential errors waiting to be exposed. Yet fear is not inevitable. The shift from fear to agency does not require sudden wealth or radical circumstance—it requires a reframing of how money decisions are perceived. When individuals begin to interpret each choice as an opportunity to exercise control and to live in alignment with their values, anxiety diminishes and confidence grows. *Money decisions stop being sites of vulnerability and become expressions of identity and intent.*

At its root, financial fear is tied to uncertainty. Most people are not trained to manage money with precision, and the complexity of modern financial products often compounds insecurity. The average individual is expected to navigate mortgages, pensions, insurance, taxation, and investment options with little formal guidance, creating a fertile ground for self-doubt. Into this uncertainty enters cultural messaging that equates mistakes with moral failure—stories of people "ruined" by debt or shamed for poor financial choices reinforce the sense that one false move can unravel security. The psychological result is paralysis: people avoid confronting their finances, delay decisions, or cling to overly conservative strategies that sacrifice growth for the illusion of safety. What begins as a rational caution becomes a chronic avoidance, fuelling more anxiety over time.

Reframing money as an arena of agency requires recognising that financial decisions, however imperfect, are rarely final verdicts. Most are adjustable, reversible, or part of a longer trajectory. The individual who invests modestly in a diversified fund, even without mastering every technicality, has exercised agency by aligning an action with the principle of future preparedness. The family that chooses to rent in order to preserve mobility rather than stretch into home ownership may resist social expectations, yet they affirm control by privileging values such as freedom and flexibility. In both cases, fear recedes because decisions are anchored not in the need to "get everything right" but in the clarity of chosen values.

Values-based reframing has profound psychological effects. Studies in behavioural finance show that people who anchor money management in personal meaning—whether it is supporting family, contributing to community, or cultivating experiences—report lower stress even when their incomes are modest. The act of linking money to values transforms transactions into expressions of identity rather than tests of competence. When someone decides to allocate funds for a sabbatical to pursue education or to dedicate a portion of income to charitable giving, the action reflects more than arithmetic; it signals intentional authorship of life. *Agency arises when money is no longer experienced solely as a measure of adequacy but as a medium of choice.*

Yet the transition is not automatic. Fear resists reframing because it is reinforced by deeply ingrained narratives. For instance, many grew up hearing warnings such as "money doesn't grow on trees" or "you must always prepare for disaster." While caution has its place, unchecked, these scripts create a worldview where scarcity is assumed and every expenditure carries the shadow of guilt. Reframing these scripts requires conscious interrogation: is the avoidance of spending aligned with one's values, or is it simply inherited fear? If values include cultivating relationships, then spending money on shared experiences may be an act of integrity rather than indulgence. If values emphasise independence, then investing in skills or tools that expand autonomy is not waste but empowerment. In this light, reframing is not about silencing fear with blind optimism; it is about *disentangling money choices from inherited anxieties and reconnecting them to self-defined priorities.*

Consider a practical example. A professional might hesitate to negotiate salary out of fear of seeming ungrateful or jeopardising a job offer. The fear frames the decision as a risk of loss. Yet reframed through the lens of agency, negotiation is an act of alignment: it asserts self-worth and communicates value to the organisation. Even if the outcome is imperfect, the act of claiming space in the financial conversation strengthens agency. The same applies to debt repayment. Approached in fear, debt looms as an unmanageable weight. Approached through agency, each payment becomes a deliberate choice to reclaim autonomy, no matter how incremental. The narrative shifts from "I am crushed by debt" to "I am directing my resources towards freedom." The numbers on the statement may remain unchanged in the short term, but the psychological landscape transforms.

Philosophically, the reframing from fear to agency recalls the broader human tension between determinism and autonomy. Fear suggests that money dictates life: that incomes, markets, and accidents impose themselves upon individuals. Agency recognises constraint but insists that choices remain. A person cannot control the economy, but they can control their spending priorities. They cannot dictate market returns, but they can decide their level of exposure. By shifting focus from what lies outside control to what can be shaped, individuals rediscover their role as agents rather than victims in financial life. This echoes the Stoic idea of directing energy towards the controllable rather than wasting it on the uncontrollable. In practical finance, this means that while one cannot banish volatility, one can set boundaries, automate behaviours, and ensure alignment with long-term values.

Importantly, agency is not the denial of risk. In fact, acknowledging risk honestly is a hallmark of agency. Fear denies risk by avoiding it, or magnifies it to paralysis. Agency accepts risk as the price of choice. For example, investing in markets carries uncertainty, but agency reframes it as participation in future growth. Insurance premiums may feel like wasted expense until reframed as an act of protecting loved ones, an expression of responsibility rather than paranoia. *Agency accepts imperfection while insisting on intentionality.* This tolerance of imperfection is central: the anxious spender or saver often clings to the fantasy of the "perfect" financial decision. Agency dismantles that fantasy by asserting that imperfect action in alignment with values is superior to perfect inaction born of fear.

The societal implications of fear versus agency are profound. Economies benefit when individuals act with agency—consuming, investing, and planning in ways that are sustainable and aligned with real needs. Fear, by contrast, distorts markets. It manifests in hoarding, panicked withdrawals, or overconsumption as individuals attempt to soothe anxiety through compulsive spending. At the macro level, fear leads to cycles of boom and bust, as collective avoidance flips into collective overreaction. At the micro level, fear erodes mental health, relationships, and opportunities for growth. Reframing money as agency not only reduces individual anxiety but also fosters healthier economic ecosystems where decisions are grounded in clarity rather than reaction.

The transition from fear to agency is, at its core, a psychological re-education. It does not eliminate financial difficulty, nor does it guarantee perpetual confidence. But it replaces paralysis with participation. It transforms the act of opening a bill, making a purchase, or planning for retirement from a confrontation with inadequacy into a demonstration of control and values. *Every financial decision becomes an opportunity to say: this is who I am, and this is what I choose to build.* In that simple but radical shift, anxiety loses its grip, replaced by the calm authority of agency.

The Role of Gratitude and Contentment – Examines how cultivating non-material satisfaction reduces destructive money behaviours

Modern consumer economies are built on restlessness. Advertising does not merely inform people about products; it works systematically to convince them that what they currently have is insufficient, outdated, or unworthy of their aspirations. The cycle thrives on discontent, promising happiness just beyond the next purchase. Yet psychological research, ancient philosophy, and lived experience all point towards the same counterintuitive truth: *gratitude and contentment do more to secure lasting financial stability than perpetual striving for more.* By cultivating non-material satisfaction, individuals reduce the impulses that lead to destructive money behaviours—overspending, compulsive upgrading, and debt-driven lifestyles—and instead reorient financial life around sufficiency, balance, and choice.

Gratitude is not a sentimental posture; it is a cognitive recalibration. Neuroscientific studies show that deliberate practices of gratitude—whether by journaling or verbal expression—shift brain activity in ways that heighten awareness of existing resources and reduce the intensity of craving. For instance, when people are guided to reflect daily on aspects of their lives for which they are grateful, including non-financial domains such as relationships or health, their reported levels of material desire diminish measurably. This is not because their circumstances change but because their perception of "enough" expands. *When the mind habitually notices sufficiency, the urge to overspend in pursuit of elusive satisfaction weakens.*

Contentment, closely allied with gratitude, is often misunderstood as resignation. In truth, it is the ability to find satisfaction without constant comparison. In financial behaviour, comparison is one of the most corrosive forces: individuals do not measure wealth in absolute terms but relative to peers, colleagues, or neighbours. A salary that once felt adequate can suddenly feel humiliating when set against the larger pay of a contemporary. Luxury goods markets depend on this psychology, marketing products as status symbols whose value derives from their exclusivity rather than their intrinsic utility. Contentment interrupts this comparison trap by anchoring value internally: it asks not "how does this compare to what others possess?" but "does this align with my needs and my principles?" This shift radically alters spending patterns. A person who buys a reliable car and feels content is shielded from the anxiety of upgrading merely because others have done so.

The practical financial consequences of gratitude and contentment are profound. Studies of household spending reveal that people who score higher on gratitude measures tend to save more consistently, carry lower credit card balances, and report less regret over financial decisions. This is not because they earn more but because they resist the impulsivity that fuels destructive money habits. The grateful consumer, more attuned to sufficiency, is less susceptible to marketing that trades on fear of missing out. The content individual avoids debt-fuelled consumption because their self-worth is not contingent on visible symbols of success. *Gratitude and contentment, though intangible qualities, produce tangible stability.*

There is also a critical emotional dimension. Destructive money behaviours are often driven by attempts to soothe discomfort. Shopping can provide a momentary dopamine surge, offering distraction from stress, loneliness, or insecurity. Yet the relief is short-lived, often followed by guilt and financial strain. Gratitude disrupts this cycle by offering a more sustainable source of emotional regulation. When one intentionally recalls the presence of supportive relationships, past achievements, or simple pleasures, the craving for external "fixes" weakens. Contentment builds on this by normalising the idea that satisfaction can be sustained without perpetual novelty. In effect, these practices inoculate against the emotional triggers that advertising and social comparison exploit.

The philosophical roots of these insights are longstanding. Ancient Stoics argued that wealth consists not in the abundance of possessions but in the ability to be satisfied with what one already has. Eastern traditions emphasise similar principles: Buddhism frames desire as a source of suffering, and contentment as liberation from its cycle. These teachings are not calls to asceticism but to agency. They suggest that when individuals choose gratitude, they regain control over financial behaviour rather than remaining captive to external pressures. Modern behavioural science, though couched in different language, corroborates this wisdom. By training attention towards sufficiency, gratitude cultivates resilience against the hedonic treadmill—the tendency to adapt rapidly to new gains, thereby neutralising their satisfaction and fuelling the demand for ever more.

Critically, gratitude and contentment do not preclude ambition. This is where scepticism often arises: if people are too content, will they cease striving, innovating, or improving? Evidence suggests otherwise. Grateful individuals are not passive; they are often more proactive in pursuing meaningful goals because they are less paralysed by envy or fear. Contentment with sufficiency does not mean rejecting growth; it means growing from a place of stability rather than compulsion. For example, someone who is grateful for their current income can still pursue a promotion—but the pursuit is framed as an opportunity to expand impact or align with values, not merely as a frantic chase to "catch up." The distinction matters: action taken from fear or inadequacy often leads to poor decisions, while action taken from contentment is more deliberate, sustainable, and aligned with long-term wellbeing.

There are practical ways to cultivate these dispositions within financial life. Gratitude can be anchored in simple rituals: recording three non-material things one is thankful for each evening, or beginning budgeting sessions by reflecting on resources already secured rather than deficits. Contentment can be reinforced through intentional pauses before spending—asking whether a purchase serves a real need or merely responds to social comparison. Introducing friction in spending, such as waiting 24 hours before discretionary purchases, can create space for gratitude to reframe perception. Over time, these practices accumulate into a mindset where sufficiency is experienced not as limitation but as liberation. *Wealth becomes less about accumulation and more about freedom from compulsion.*

At the societal level, gratitude and contentment challenge the dominant narrative that economic growth and individual consumption are the primary routes to fulfilment. While growth has lifted millions from poverty, its cultural by-products—status competition, planned obsolescence, consumer debt—have also generated widespread insecurity. A culture that privileges gratitude is one that celebrates sufficiency and sustainability. It values financial prudence without equating frugality with deprivation. It recognises that true wealth lies in the ability to direct resources towards meaningful ends, not in the endless multiplication of goods. Contentment, similarly, redefines success not as perpetual escalation but as alignment between means and values. If more individuals adopted this orientation, the collective demand for conspicuous consumption would diminish, easing ecological strain and enhancing communal wellbeing.

Perhaps the most radical impact of gratitude and contentment lies in their ability to restore dignity. Financial anxiety often erodes self-esteem, leaving individuals feeling perpetually behind. Gratitude interrupts this by reframing what has already been achieved. The individual with modest savings but consistent support from friends and family can see themselves not as "failing" but as already rich in ways that matter. Contentment reinforces this dignity by affirming that self-worth is not hostage to comparison. This is not an excuse for complacency; rather, it is a recognition that destructive money behaviours lose their grip when individuals no longer equate their identity with their purchasing power.

By cultivating gratitude and contentment, people gain more than emotional serenity; they acquire a stabilising force against the pressures of modern finance. They spend with discernment rather than compulsion, save with consistency rather than panic, and invest with patience rather than desperation. *Non-material satisfaction is not peripheral to financial health—it is its foundation.* Without it, even high earners remain trapped in cycles of fear and craving. With it, even modest incomes can yield a life experienced as abundant. Gratitude and contentment, properly understood, are not luxuries but essential disciplines—disciplines that transform the psychology of money from a battlefield of insecurity into a practice of sufficiency and choice.

Wealth as a Practice – Positions financial well-being not as a destination but as an ongoing, mindful set of practices

The dominant cultural script treats wealth as a static condition, a threshold to be crossed or a destination to be reached. The language itself betrays this fixation: people speak of *becoming wealthy* or *achieving financial success*, as though wealth were a fixed address at which one finally arrives and thereafter remains. Yet this framing obscures the reality that financial well-being is not a singular event but a continual practice. Like physical health, it cannot be "achieved" once and for all; it must be sustained through habits, vigilance, and adaptability. *Wealth is not a product of what one has but of how one manages, interprets, and integrates resources over time.*

One of the most striking findings from longitudinal studies on wealth accumulation is that sudden inflows of money—whether through inheritance, windfalls, or lottery winnings—rarely guarantee long-term prosperity. Within a few years, many recipients of windfalls return to their pre-existing financial condition, sometimes worse off than before. The explanation lies not in the size of the capital but in the practices surrounding it. Without disciplined spending, structured saving, and an orientation towards long-term goals, large sums evaporate under the pressure of immediate consumption or poor investment. Conversely, modest earners who embed consistent habits—automatic savings, cautious debt management, deliberate consumption—can accumulate stability and security far beyond what their income level might suggest. *It is not wealth that produces good practice, but good practice that sustains and expands wealth.*

This distinction matters because it reframes wealth as agency rather than accumulation. If wealth were merely a matter of reaching a numerical target—say, a certain salary or net worth—then it would be inherently precarious, forever subject to loss through crisis, inflation, or misfortune. But when wealth is seen as a practice, it becomes a set of behaviours and attitudes that can be enacted regardless of circumstance. Someone who tracks expenses with clarity, aligns spending with values, and maintains a margin of safety is already "wealthy" in practice, even if their balance sheet is modest. By contrast, someone with vast resources but no capacity to steward them mindfully is vulnerable to sudden collapse.

Understanding wealth as practice also allows us to disentangle it from income. The assumption that higher earnings automatically generate financial security is contradicted by evidence: many professionals with six-figure salaries live from paycheck to paycheck, constrained by debt, lifestyle inflation, and social pressure. Their income, while large, does not translate into resilience. Meanwhile, households with half that income but stronger practices of budgeting, delayed gratification, and intentional consumption build real security. This explains why surveys consistently find a disconnect between income and financial satisfaction. Wealth, properly conceived, is less about scale and more about sustainability. *It is a rhythm, not a result.*

To cultivate wealth as practice requires a shift from outcome-based goals to process-based commitments. An outcome goal might be to accumulate a certain retirement balance by age sixty. A process goal, by contrast, is to contribute a consistent percentage of income to long-term savings, regardless of fluctuations. Outcome goals can motivate but also discourage when setbacks occur. Process goals, rooted in habit, are more resilient. They harness the power of compounding: small, repeated actions build systems that run even when motivation falters. The person who automates a modest transfer into an investment account each month is less dependent on willpower than the one who waits to save "what's left over."

Philosophically, this orientation aligns with traditions that emphasise discipline as liberation. The Stoics argued that freedom arises not from external circumstances but from mastery over one's responses. Financially, wealth as practice reflects the same principle: it is not the fluctuating tides of markets or salaries that determine one's condition, but the habits enacted daily. This perspective also undermines the corrosive myth of arrival—the belief that one can simply earn or save enough to eliminate all future anxiety. Even at high levels of affluence, individuals remain susceptible to insecurity if their financial life lacks practice. They fear loss, they chase comparison, they overspend to maintain appearances. Without mindful engagement, money becomes a source of fragility rather than freedom.

Critically, wealth as practice is not only defensive but creative. It enables choice. A person who has cultivated practices of saving, budgeting, and aligning spending with values can redirect resources towards opportunities—education, entrepreneurship, philanthropy—without jeopardising stability. This dynamic quality of wealth as practice makes it expansive: it grows not simply by accumulating but by opening space for meaningful decisions. For example, an employee who has built a modest emergency fund and structured their spending can take the risk of leaving an unfulfilling job to retrain or start a business. Their financial practice provides not just safety but agency. *The practice of wealth enlarges life beyond the numbers.*

Modern behavioural economics supports this framing. Default bias—the tendency to stick with pre-set options—means that systems matter more than intentions. When individuals design their financial environment so that good practices are automatic, wealth becomes less about heroic acts of discipline and more about structural support. For example, enrolling in automatic retirement contributions or setting up a spending account with fixed limits reduces reliance on constant decision-making. This aligns with the recognition that willpower is finite; practice succeeds where discipline alone fails. Wealth is not preserved through occasional bursts of austerity but through embedded systems that make the prudent choice the easiest one.

The view of wealth as practice also addresses the psychological component of financial well-being. Anxiety often stems from uncertainty, not scarcity. Two households with identical resources may experience radically different levels of stress depending on whether they feel in control of their practices. One may live in constant fear of the next bill, the other in calm assurance that their systems anticipate and manage such events. Contentment, too, is cultivated through practice: the regular act of aligning spending with values, reflecting on sufficiency, and reinforcing gratitude builds a sense of wealth independent of external benchmarks. This mental wealth, grounded in habit, protects against the corrosive effects of comparison and advertising.

Importantly, positioning wealth as practice also reframes intergenerational dynamics. Parents who leave large inheritances without teaching financial practices often unintentionally sow instability. By contrast, parents who model budgeting, saving, and value-based consumption equip children with practices that endure across lifetimes, regardless of the initial financial base. In this sense, the most valuable inheritance is not a sum of money but a set of financial practices that secure resilience and autonomy. *Wealth is sustained not by capital alone but by the transmission of practice.*

To see wealth in this way is to demystify it. The mythology of "becoming wealthy" often paralyses individuals, convincing them that security lies forever out of reach until some dramatic change occurs—an inheritance, a higher salary, a lucrative investment. The truth is more accessible and more demanding: wealth is already available to anyone willing to cultivate practices of attention, discipline, and alignment. It does not eliminate uncertainty or erase risk, but it transforms the relationship to them. Wealth as practice means approaching money not as a finish line but as a daily craft, honed over time.

By adopting this perspective, individuals free themselves from the illusion that wealth is a scarce prize reserved for a lucky few. They recognise it instead as a set of patterns available to anyone willing to engage consistently. The practice may be unglamorous—logging expenses, automating transfers, resisting comparison—but its cumulative effect is profound. Over years, these practices yield stability, choice, and peace of mind, which are the true markers of financial well-being. In this light, *wealth ceases to be a possession and becomes a discipline*—a way of living with money that continually creates, preserves, and renews freedom.

Chapter 11
A Different Kind of Rich

Across cultures and generations, wealth has been imagined as a number, a status, a measurable attainment visible on spreadsheets and in lifestyles. But what if richness is not captured by accumulation at all? What if the truest forms of prosperity resist simple accounting and instead reside in qualities such as stability, autonomy, and the integrity of living in alignment with one's values? To ask this question is to challenge the very architecture of modern financial aspiration. For too long, the conversation about wealth has been framed in purely quantitative terms, reducing lives to balances and portfolios, as if the worth of existence could be condensed into a line item. Yet history and psychology alike suggest otherwise: material abundance, when detached from meaning, does little to sustain fulfilment, and in many cases magnifies anxiety. A different kind of rich is not defined by how much is owned, but by the extent to which money serves life rather than dominates it.

This reframing requires us to interrogate the narratives that shape economic ambition. The cultural archetype of success—luxury possessions, escalating consumption, and financial outperformance of one's peers—has been marketed so relentlessly that it has become almost invisible, absorbed as common sense. But the price of this model is clear. Countless individuals spend decades chasing symbols of prosperity, only to discover that they remain insecure, perpetually striving, and often alienated from themselves. At the heart of this paradox lies a conceptual error: confusing the capacity to acquire with the capacity to live well. Stability, freedom of choice, and the coherence between financial decisions and personal values are far more reliable indicators of well-being than raw income or net worth. A person who has enough to meet obligations, cushion against volatility, and make deliberate decisions is, in practical terms, wealthier than someone with far greater resources but no sense of control or alignment.

Seeing money as a tool rather than a master is central to this alternative understanding. Tools exist to extend human capability, to enable projects, relationships, and contributions that would otherwise remain impossible. Yet many individuals unconsciously invert this relationship, becoming tools of their money—working ever harder, making choices dictated by financial status, or measuring their self-worth against arbitrary benchmarks. The reorientation begins with a deceptively simple shift: asking not "How much can I get?" but "What is this money for?" Such a question restores purpose to the financial domain. Money, untethered from purpose, becomes performative; tethered to life, it becomes liberating. Consider the professional who reduces working hours, accepting lower pay, to spend more time with family or pursue creative work. Though their income diminishes, their sense of richness expands, because money has been positioned in service to values rather than in opposition to them.

Taking the long view deepens this redefinition. The conventional financial horizon is narrow, dominated by short-term gains, immediate gratification, and comparison against present peers. But when one extends the horizon—thinking in decades rather than months, considering generational consequences rather than seasonal appearances—the shape of financial decisions changes. Short-term sacrifice for long-term resilience becomes intelligible rather than punishing. For example, investing consistently in skills or relationships may yield little immediate status but proves invaluable over time. Environmental sustainability, too, is illuminated by this lens: decisions made today, even at personal cost, acquire meaning when framed as contributions to a habitable future. The long view is both pragmatic and philosophical; it anchors individuals in a continuity of time that stretches beyond their immediate wants, embedding their financial choices in a larger narrative of sustainability and legacy.

That legacy, in turn, reveals the cultural significance of rewriting the "money mind." For too long, wealth transmission has been conceived primarily in terms of inheritance—assets handed down, estates settled, fortunes divided. Yet the deeper legacy is psychological and behavioural. The attitudes towards money, the practices of stewardship, the narratives of what constitutes success—all of these are absorbed by children and communities, shaping financial culture across generations. To cultivate a different kind of rich is therefore not only an act of personal liberation but of cultural transformation. Parents who model mindful spending, purposeful saving, and value-driven choices transmit far more than financial capital; they transmit frameworks of meaning. Colleagues, students, and peers similarly absorb alternative definitions of success when they encounter them embodied. The result is a ripple effect in which redefining richness at the individual level subtly reshapes the collective imagination.

The promise of this chapter lies in its invitation to think differently about what it means to prosper. Rather than surrendering to the treadmill of "more"—more income, more possessions, more comparisons—it suggests that true richness lies in sufficiency with agency, in freedom without compulsion, and in financial choices that reinforce rather than undermine identity. It asks readers to consider the possibility that wealth measured purely by accumulation is a fragile illusion, and that the deeper, more resilient kind of wealth is one that endures across contexts, supports stability, and aligns with what matters most. By engaging with these ideas, readers are not only offered strategies for personal financial well-being, but a lens through which to participate in redefining what their communities, families, and future generations will understand as prosperity. This is not a minor shift in emphasis; it is a fundamental reorientation. To be "a different kind of rich" is not simply to have money, but to master the art of living with it wisely, purposefully, and with an eye toward the enduring rather than the fleeting.

Redefining Success

Few concepts are as widely accepted yet as rarely interrogated as the idea of success. In much of the modern world, its meaning has been compressed into the language of accumulation: more income, more possessions, more visibility of achievement. Success, in this framework, is measured by what can be counted—salaries, homes, assets, awards. But what if this metric, so deeply embedded in culture, education, and aspiration, is not only inadequate but actively misleading? The assumption that accumulation equates to prosperity reduces human lives to financial statements and perpetuates an arms race of comparison that few can ever truly win. It ignores the evidence—psychological, sociological, and historical—that beyond a certain threshold of material comfort, the connection between "more" and "better" frays, leaving individuals wealthier in numbers but poorer in stability, freedom, and fulfilment.

To redefine success is not to diminish ambition but to expand its frame. The accumulation model is compelling because it offers clarity: more is always measurable. Yet clarity and truth are not the same. A broader definition demands that we recognise *wealth as sufficiency plus choice*. Sufficiency ensures that basic needs are met and vulnerabilities are buffered; choice provides the freedom to align decisions with one's own values rather than with external pressures. Stability, in this sense, becomes a more valuable currency than growth. Consider the employee who chooses a role with moderate pay but a supportive work culture, long-term security, and alignment with personal passions. Conventional metrics might categorise them as less successful than a peer with a higher salary but relentless burnout. Yet over time, stability generates a richer quality of life, protecting health, relationships, and psychological well-being. Success, then, emerges less from the scale of earnings than from the coherence between financial life and personal values.

Historical patterns reinforce this reframing. Across societies, those who are remembered not simply as wealthy but as prosperous are rarely those who hoarded the greatest fortunes. Instead, they are individuals or groups who embedded money within broader purposes—building institutions, supporting communities, or cultivating the conditions for stability in times of volatility. The Roman notion of *otium*—leisure devoted to reflection, creativity, and civic engagement—contrasted with mere *negotium*, the endless pursuit of business and gain. Similarly, indigenous traditions in parts of Africa and North America viewed wealth less as accumulation than as distribution: the ability to give, sustain, and contribute defined status more than what was owned privately. These cultural lenses remind us that accumulation is only one story of wealth, and often the least enduring.

The psychological dimension of redefining success is equally critical. Modern economies cultivate an environment where anxiety is the by-product of aspiration. Even among high earners, surveys show widespread financial stress—not because resources are lacking, but because comparison sets the benchmark infinitely higher. If a neighbour's home or colleague's promotion recalibrates one's sense of adequacy, the pursuit of success becomes a treadmill without destination. By contrast, when success is defined by stability, freedom, and alignment, the goalposts stop shifting with every external cue. An individual who sets aside savings not to outshine peers but to ensure resilience against unexpected change experiences their financial life not as fragile but as empowering. *Success becomes self-referential, not socially dictated.*

Case studies highlight this difference. Consider the Scandinavian model, often cited in debates about prosperity. These societies, despite having high taxation and limited extremes of wealth, consistently rank among the world's happiest. The reason lies less in sheer income levels than in the stability and freedom their systems provide: universal healthcare, strong worker protections, and a cultural emphasis on balance rather than relentless accumulation. The lesson is not that Scandinavian structures can simply be replicated elsewhere, but that redefining success around sufficiency and alignment produces measurable improvements in well-being. By contrast, in nations where accumulation dominates cultural narratives, rising GDP often coincides with rising inequality and declining satisfaction, showing the limits of growth as the sole metric of prosperity.

Yet it is not only at the societal level that this redefinition matters. On an individual scale, financial stability and alignment create a foundation for values-driven decision-making. Professionals who step off high-pressure career tracks to pursue vocations aligned with meaning frequently report greater satisfaction even when their income drops. Entrepreneurs who choose sustainable business models over extractive ones may grow more slowly but enjoy resilience and long-term impact. Parents who prioritise time with children over acquiring larger homes embody a richness that is invisible in economic statistics but palpable in lived experience. These examples underscore that freedom—the capacity to choose according to values—is a far more accurate barometer of success than accumulation, which often limits choice by binding individuals to obligations, debt, or relentless performance.

Of course, this redefinition is not without its tensions. Advocates of traditional accumulation models argue that wealth creates security, opportunity, and influence, all of which can be deployed for good. There is truth here: financial resources do expand possibilities. Yet when accumulation is pursued without regard for stability or alignment, the trade-offs can become destructive. A high-paying role that erodes health, a growing portfolio that consumes attention and time, a lifestyle built on comparison rather than choice—all of these create vulnerabilities masked by financial abundance. The tension, then, is not between accumulation and sufficiency but between accumulation as an end in itself and accumulation as a means to freedom and alignment. Redefining success requires asking at every stage: *Does this increase serve stability and values, or does it destabilise them?*

Philosophically, this shift demands courage. To measure success differently is to resist dominant narratives, to opt out of the comparisons that saturate media, workplaces, and even family dynamics. It requires cultivating an internal locus of wealth, where prosperity is defined by the life one is able to live rather than by the metrics others use to judge it. In practice, this might mean celebrating milestones that rarely appear in financial headlines: the month a person finally pays off debt and experiences peace of mind, the year they structure work around health needs rather than around maximising profit, or the decision to invest in friendships, community, and personal growth rather than in conspicuous consumption. These choices, while modest in financial terms, are profound markers of redefined success.

Ultimately, redefining success reshapes both ambition and legacy. Ambition is no longer about reaching the highest rung of accumulation but about constructing a life that is stable, free, and coherent with values. Legacy shifts from being measured solely in assets transferred to being measured in models of living passed down: children who inherit not only money but healthy attitudes toward it, communities that internalise sufficiency as a virtue, societies that value stability as much as growth. By stepping beyond accumulation as the default, individuals and cultures alike reclaim success as something deeply human: the art of living in a way that is sustainable, free, and aligned with what matters most.

To embrace this definition is to resist reductionism, to refuse to flatten prosperity into numbers. It is to recognise that *the richest life is not the one with the most, but the one lived with enough and with choice.* This is not an abandonment of financial aspiration but its elevation, moving from a narrow obsession with accumulation to a holistic vision of what it means to thrive.

Money in Service of Life

Money is perhaps the most versatile invention humanity has created, yet it is also the most easily misunderstood. At its core, money is a system of exchange—an elegant tool designed to simplify trade, reduce uncertainty, and expand the possibilities of human cooperation. Yet across centuries it has acquired a distorted role, evolving from servant to master, from instrument to idol. When money ceases to be a means and becomes the measure of worth in itself, people do not use it to enhance life but instead shape life to serve it. The result is a society where performance eclipses purpose, where individuals confuse the accumulation of currency with the creation of meaning. To return money to its rightful place—as a tool in service of life—is one of the most urgent challenges of our age.

One of the paradoxes of modern affluence is that those with the greatest financial resources often report the least sense of freedom. Studies consistently show that after a certain threshold—enough to cover security and modest comforts—additional income does little to increase happiness, and yet the pursuit of "more" intensifies. This is not irrationality but conditioning. Cultures steeped in competition and comparison equate financial performance with identity and success. The banker who earns millions but works eighty hours a week, neglecting health and family, is praised as successful, while the teacher who earns moderately but lives with stability and purpose is dismissed as merely average. The distortion lies not in money itself but in the narratives surrounding it: the belief that money is the goal, not the means to something larger.

Reframing money as a tool requires clarity about what it should serve. At the individual level, this means asking whether financial choices reflect values or anxieties. When money is treated as performance, decisions often arise from fear of falling behind or from the need to signal status. This leads to behaviours such as overspending to keep pace with peers or underspending out of chronic insecurity, both of which diminish life rather than enrich it. But when money is placed in service of life, decisions are filtered through the lens of purpose: does this expenditure, investment, or saving move me closer to the life I value? Does it expand my ability to act in alignment with what matters, or does it tether me to obligations that contradict it?

Practical examples illustrate this shift. Consider the growing movement towards "financial independence, retire early" (FIRE). While the name suggests early exit from work, its deeper philosophy is about freedom: structuring money to serve life rather than to prolong endless employment. Participants aggressively save not for hoarding's sake but to buy back time, autonomy, and alignment with personal priorities. By contrast, those who accumulate wealth without a sense of purpose often find themselves trapped in what economists call the "hedonic treadmill"—higher income leading to higher consumption, leaving satisfaction unchanged. In the former case, money serves; in the latter, money dictates.

The distinction becomes sharper when we consider social contexts. When money serves life, communities flourish. Resources are directed not only towards private gain but towards shared infrastructure, education, health, and art—all investments in human flourishing. When money becomes a master, it drives inequality, hoarding, and short-term exploitation. One only needs to observe how societies with strong safety nets and civic investments generate greater life satisfaction than those with stark inequality, despite comparable GDP. The difference lies in the role money plays: in one, it is a means to stability and collective well-being; in the other, it is an end in itself.

Philosophically, treating money as a tool realigns it with the broader tradition of purpose-driven living. Aristotle argued that wealth is not the good we seek but only useful for the sake of something else—friendship, virtue, contemplation. In modern terms, this translates to recognising that while money enables choice, it cannot define meaning. A holiday with loved ones, the ability to pursue a vocation aligned with values, the freedom to contribute to causes larger than oneself—these are the ends money can serve, but they lose value when money itself becomes the measure. *To make money the master is to invert means and ends, and this inversion generates anxiety, emptiness, and perpetual dissatisfaction.*

Critically, money as servant is not an abstract ideal but a practical framework for decision-making. It demands structures that tether money to values. For example, automating savings towards goals that genuinely matter—a child's education, time for creative pursuits, or a safety buffer for health—ensures that money is channelled into life-serving functions rather than dissipated through unconscious consumption. Similarly, introducing deliberate "friction" in spending—such as waiting periods for non-essential purchases—shifts money from impulse to intention. These tools demonstrate that when money is disciplined by values, it enhances freedom rather than constrains it.

Yet the shift also requires a cultural unlearning. In many professions, identity is fused with financial performance: the lawyer who equates billable hours with value, the entrepreneur whose worth is tied to valuation. To see money as a servant rather than a master demands courage to resist these metrics and redefine what counts as achievement. It may involve choosing less lucrative work that aligns with health, relationships, and contribution. It may mean embracing sufficiency rather than endless growth. This is not resignation but agency: the power to shape life rather than be shaped by financial performance. *True wealth lies not in the scale of accumulation but in the coherence between money and meaning.*

The legacy dimension is equally profound. How we relate to money does not stop with us; it is transmitted through family, institutions, and culture. Parents who model money as performance raise children primed for anxiety and comparison. Parents who model money as a tool raise children who see it as a resource for stability, freedom, and purpose. Institutions that equate success with quarterly earnings perpetuate short-term exploitation; institutions that define success in terms of sustainable contribution cultivate resilience. In this sense, each individual and organisation that reframes money from master to servant contributes to rewriting the cultural "money mind" itself.

The ultimate irony is that money, when treated as an end, often fails to deliver even the security it promises. Markets shift, fortunes erode, and careers change. But money that has been consciously placed in service of life—structured for sufficiency, aligned with values, deployed for stability—produces resilience even in uncertainty. It allows individuals to navigate change without losing coherence, because their foundation is not the quantity of money but its orientation. Stability and meaning are portable in a way raw accumulation never is.

To encourage money as a tool rather than a master is to reassert human agency over one of our most powerful inventions. It is to remember that money has no inherent purpose apart from what we assign to it. By anchoring financial decisions in values, freedom, and purpose, we transform money from a source of anxiety and distortion into a resource for flourishing. This reorientation does not diminish the importance of money but restores it to its rightful place: a servant that, when wisely directed, amplifies life rather than governs it.

The Long View

Modern culture often trains us to think in days, weeks, or at best quarters, while the most meaningful outcomes of our financial lives unfold across decades. This short-term orientation is not accidental. Markets are reported in daily fluctuations, companies are evaluated by quarterly earnings, and individuals are encouraged to measure success in immediate consumption or visible signs of prosperity. Yet the consequences of such narrow horizons are profound: debt spirals begin with today's small indulgence, retirement crises with years of under-saving, and environmental degradation with decisions made for next year's profit. Reframing our relationship with money through the lens of the long view challenges this default mode of thinking. It invites us to measure not simply what our resources do for us now but what they enable across the full arc of life.

One of the most striking findings in behavioural finance is the extent to which humans discount the future. Psychologists call this "present bias"—our tendency to overvalue immediate rewards relative to delayed ones. This bias explains why someone might spend lavishly on a night out while deferring retirement savings, even though the latter has far greater long-term significance. The long view disrupts this bias by reframing decisions in terms of their enduring consequences. Instead of asking, "What do I gain today?" the more powerful question becomes, "What trajectory am I setting in motion?" This shift turns money decisions from discrete transactions into components of a narrative, where each choice is a chapter influencing the ending.

Consider the difference in perspective between someone who views housing purely as consumption—choosing the maximum mortgage they qualify for because it secures immediate comfort—and someone who sees housing as part of a thirty-year strategy. The latter may select a smaller home, not out of deprivation, but because it creates surplus cash flow that compounds into savings, investments, and freedom. Over decades, the second approach not only builds resilience but reduces stress, as life is not perpetually stretched to the financial limit. *The long view transforms restraint into empowerment: it is not about what is denied today, but what is enabled tomorrow.*

This principle extends beyond personal finance into broader societal issues. When corporations operate on quarterly earnings pressures, decisions are skewed towards immediate profitability even at the expense of sustainability. Investment in employee development, research, or environmental responsibility often loses out to short-term shareholder returns. Yet the companies that endure—those that build reputations, trust, and adaptive capacity—are those that manage to balance present needs with long-term stewardship. The lesson is not confined to the corporate world. Individuals too are stewards: of families, communities, and futures. To live only for the present is to mortgage the future; to see the long view is to practise stewardship across generations.

Importantly, adopting the long view does not mean suppressing present enjoyment. It means aligning present actions with future coherence. A holiday, when framed as indulgence, can undermine long-term goals; but when integrated into a balanced financial plan, it supports well-being and sustainability. The distinction lies in intentionality. Without the long view, present spending is often reactionary—a relief from stress, an imitation of peers, an escape from insecurity. With the long view, present spending is strategic, chosen because it contributes to both current satisfaction and long-term stability. *The most sustainable financial lives are those where today's pleasures do not sabotage tomorrow's security.*

Philosophically, the long view reintroduces time as an ethical dimension of money. If money is power, then how we wield it today shapes not only our own future but that of others. Climate change offers the starkest example. Choosing cheap, unsustainable options may yield immediate savings but at the cost of environmental degradation that future generations must bear. The long view forces us to acknowledge such externalities, reminding us that financial decisions are never isolated—they ripple forward in time. In this sense, the long view is not only a strategy but a moral orientation, cultivating responsibility towards outcomes we may never live to see.

The psychological benefits are equally significant. Anxiety around money often stems from short-term focus: the bills due this week, the investments fluctuating this month, the salary negotiation this year. These immediate pressures can dominate attention and distort judgement. By contrast, adopting a long horizon reframes temporary setbacks as episodes in a larger story. A market downturn ceases to be a crisis and becomes a chapter in a decades-long investment plan. A career plateau is seen not as failure but as one point in a trajectory that may later include reinvention and growth. *The long view introduces perspective, and perspective is one of the most powerful antidotes to financial anxiety.*

Case studies of successful long-term investors highlight the same principle. Warren Buffett is often celebrated not for his extraordinary stock-picking skill but for his patience—the willingness to let compounding unfold over half a century. Similarly, pension funds that resisted short-term panic during recessions recovered not by clever manoeuvres but by simply staying aligned with the long view. These examples underscore a broader truth: compounding, whether financial or psychological, rewards patience. The difficulty is not intellectual—most people understand compounding—but emotional. It requires resisting the noise of the present long enough to let time work its quiet magic.

Yet it would be naïve to present the long view as universally easy. For individuals living in precarity, the future can feel inaccessible. When resources barely cover present needs, saving for decades ahead seems absurd. Here lies one of the great social challenges: without systemic supports, only the privileged can afford the long view. Policies that provide healthcare, education, and basic security expand the capacity of citizens to plan beyond tomorrow. Thus, the long view is not only a matter of individual discipline but of collective design. A society that enables its members to think long-term is one that fosters stability, innovation, and intergenerational fairness.

At the personal level, cultivating the long view often begins with small rituals. Journaling about financial goals over five, ten, or twenty years. Setting automated contributions towards retirement, so that saving becomes habitual rather than optional. Building friction into spending decisions—waiting seventy-two hours before large purchases—to see whether they align with long-term priorities. These practices rewire the brain to associate money not merely with immediate gratification but with enduring security and freedom. Over time, such habits accumulate into a mindset shift: present decisions feel incomplete unless their long-term consequences are considered.

The long view also changes how we interpret success. In a short-term frame, success is earning more this year than last, or spending more conspicuously than peers. In the long view, success is measured by sustainability: whether one can withstand shocks, whether one's financial life supports values across decades, whether decisions made today would still appear wise in hindsight twenty years hence. This is a subtler, quieter form of success—less visible in displays of consumption but far more enduring in the peace of mind it delivers. *Sustainability, not speed, becomes the true measure of financial wisdom.*

Ultimately, the long view is an invitation to live in alignment with time itself. Life is not a series of disconnected moments but a continuum, and money is most powerful when integrated into that continuum. To see only the present is to be enslaved by it; to see only the distant future is to neglect the joy of now. The art lies in holding both: crafting a financial life where today's actions are meaningful in themselves and coherent with what one hopes the future will be. In that balance, money ceases to be a source of tension between present and future selves and becomes instead a bridge, carrying values forward across the decades.

Leaving a New Legacy

Every family, whether it acknowledges it or not, carries a financial culture. It may be visible in the way parents speak about money, in the habits of saving or spending that echo across generations, or in the unspoken assumptions children absorb long before they open their first bank account. For some, that legacy is one of prudence, stability, and opportunity; for others, it is marked by scarcity, secrecy, or excess. What is often overlooked is that this inheritance is not limited to property, investments, or debt. *The most enduring legacy we pass on is not what sits in our accounts, but the mindset through which future generations come to view money itself.*

Legacy is commonly framed in material terms—wills, estates, inheritances—but the subtler legacy of beliefs and behaviours shapes lives just as powerfully. A family that equates wealth with worth transmits a burden of performance that can haunt its descendants. A household where financial hardship was met with silence may foster anxiety that lingers for decades. Conversely, families that treat money as a tool for security, freedom, and generosity cultivate resilience across generations. When we speak of rewriting the "money mind," therefore, the stakes extend beyond the individual. We are setting the blueprint for those who come after us.

Historical patterns illustrate how cultural money scripts echo across time. Immigrant families, for example, often emphasise frugality and sacrifice, born from the precariousness of their early years. That frugality can evolve into a strength, instilling discipline and resourcefulness, but it can also calcify into fear, leading later generations to hoard rather than invest. Similarly, families that experienced sudden prosperity may pass on habits of display, seeking status through consumption, a pattern that erodes stability over time. These examples reveal how legacies are not static. They evolve, sometimes distorting original intentions. *The challenge of legacy is not whether it will exist but what form it will take—and whether we are intentional in shaping it.*

To leave a new legacy requires conscious disruption of inherited scripts. This is not always easy, as money habits are rarely neutral; they are entangled with identity, values, and emotional history. A parent who grew up in scarcity may overcompensate by shielding their children from financial realities, inadvertently leaving them ill-prepared for adult responsibilities. Breaking such cycles begins with awareness: recognising that patterns which once served survival may no longer serve flourishing. Rewriting legacy is not an act of condemnation of the past but an act of stewardship for the future.

Practical steps illustrate how such transformation unfolds. Parents who involve children in discussions about budgeting, even at a simple level, transmit transparency rather than secrecy. Adults who frame philanthropy as part of family life model generosity not as occasional charity but as an ongoing ethic. Couples who articulate shared financial values—whether prioritising education, sustainability, or time—offer their children a lived example that money is not just about accumulation but about alignment. *Each of these practices plants seeds: what is modelled today becomes the default tomorrow.*

The corporate world provides a parallel lesson. Just as organisations cultivate cultures around profit, risk, and responsibility, families cultivate cultures around money. A company that prioritises long-term investment in people over short-term extraction is remembered for its legacy of sustainability. Families face the same choice: will they be remembered for patterns of anxiety and conflict, or for fostering security and agency? This perspective reframes legacy from inheritance as an event to legacy as a practice, lived daily in habits, conversations, and decisions.

There is also a societal dimension. The way we manage our personal financial lives contributes to collective norms. When individuals normalise conspicuous consumption, it elevates social pressure for others to conform, entrenching a culture of status-seeking. By contrast, when individuals normalise financial mindfulness—living within means, practising generosity, investing in community—they contribute to a culture of responsibility. In this sense, personal choices reverberate outward. They influence peers, colleagues, and networks, shaping not only family legacy but societal legacy. The ripple effect is powerful: a new legacy does not end with one household; it alters the broader financial ecosystem.

Philosophically, legacy touches on mortality. Money is the part of our lives most likely to outlive us, whether through assets, debts, or the memory of how we handled it. Yet legacy is not about permanence but about continuity. What persists is not the specific numbers in accounts but the values and frameworks we transmit. A child who inherits a modest estate but a robust sense of financial agency is richer than one who inherits wealth without wisdom. *The deepest form of wealth is knowledge passed on in usable, lived form.*

The act of leaving a new legacy, then, is both personal and cultural. It requires individuals to examine their money mind honestly, to identify which parts they wish to preserve and which to transform. It demands courage to resist inherited narratives, whether of scarcity, excess, or silence. It also requires humility, acknowledging that legacy is not control—it is influence. Once transmitted, it will be reshaped by those who receive it. But influence matters. By planting healthier scripts, we alter what future generations have to work with.

This reframing invites us to think expansively. If legacy is not limited to heirs, then it includes communities, institutions, and even the planet. Financial choices about consumption, investment, and sustainability determine not only family outcomes but collective ones. To prioritise short-term gain at the expense of long-term stability is to leave a legacy of fragility. To integrate values of responsibility, stewardship, and fairness is to leave a legacy of resilience. In this sense, rewriting the money mind is a civic as well as a personal act.

Ultimately, the question each of us faces is not whether we will leave a legacy, but what kind it will be. The choice is between transmitting default scripts shaped by fear, status, or avoidance, or cultivating new scripts centred on autonomy, sufficiency, and values. The legacy of financial culture is not etched in stone; it is written, line by line, in the ways we earn, spend, save, give, and teach. By choosing with awareness, we do more than secure our own lives. We shape the financial imaginations of those who follow, ensuring that the wealth we pass on is not merely material but cultural, ethical, and sustainable.

About the Author

Nico Farouq writes about the hidden forces that drive our financial lives, blending psychology, culture, and personal finance into clear, practical insights. His work focuses on the unseen habits and beliefs that determine why people succeed or struggle with money, even when they earn well. Known for his ability to translate complex research into everyday wisdom, Farouq challenges readers to see money not just as numbers, but as a mirror of values, identity, and choice. His earlier book, Mission-Driven Money: How Purpose Fuels Profit, explored how aligning finance with purpose creates sustainable wealth. In this new work, he turns inward—revealing the unconscious scripts that keep people stuck and showing how to rewrite them for freedom and balance.

www.ingramcontent.com/pod-product-compliance
Lightning Source LLC
Chambersburg PA
CBHW031346230926
51848CB00002B/404
9789371775953